Paddling Kentucky

Paddling
Kentucky

A Guide to the State's Best Paddling Adventures

Carrie Stambaugh

GUILFORD, CONNECTICUT

An imprint of The Rowman & Littlefield Publishing Group, Inc.
4501 Forbes Blvd., Ste. 200
Lanham, MD 20706
www.rowman.com

Falcon and FalconGuides are registered trademarks and Make Adventure Your Story is a trademark of The Rowman & Littlefield Publishing Group, Inc.

Distributed by NATIONAL BOOK NETWORK

Copyright © 2019 The Rowman & Littlefield Publishing Group, Inc.
Maps by The Rowman & Littlefield Publishing Group, Inc.

British Library Cataloguing in Publication Information available

Library of Congress Cataloging-in-Publication Data available

ISBN 978-1-4930-2438-4 (paperback)
ISBN 978-1-4930-2439-1 (e-book)

∞™ The paper used in this publication meets the minimum requirements of American National Standard for Information Sciences—Permanence of Paper for Printed Library Materials, ANSI/NISO Z39.48-1992.

Printed in the United States of America

The author and The Rowman & Littlefield Publishing Group, Inc., assume no liability for accidents happening to, or injuries sustained by, readers who engage in the activities described in this book.

In memory of Carl Edward Stambaugh
July 22, 1944–October 20, 2017

The Palisades rise above a rapid along Dix River a mile upstream from its confluence with the Kentucky River. CARRIE STAMBAUGH

Contents

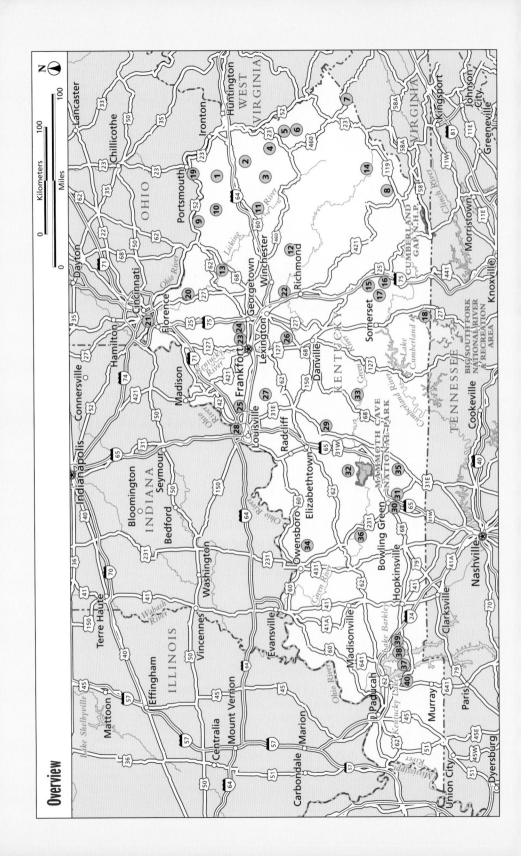

Map Legend

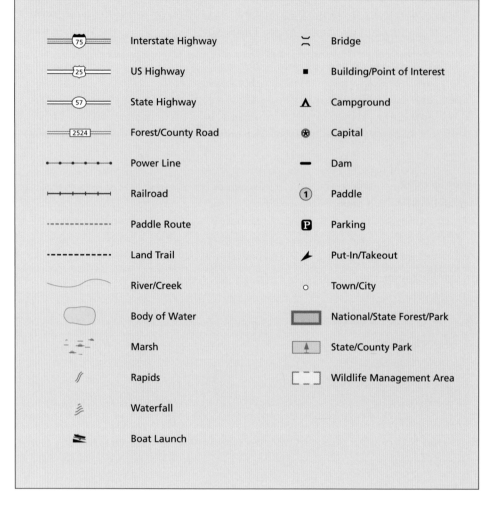

Interstate Highway	Bridge
US Highway	Building/Point of Interest
State Highway	Campground
Forest/County Road	Capital
Power Line	Dam
Railroad	Paddle
Paddle Route	Parking
Land Trail	Put-In/Takeout
River/Creek	Town/City
Body of Water	National/State Forest/Park
Marsh	State/County Park
Rapids	Wildlife Management Area
Waterfall	
Boat Launch	

Acknowledgments

I am grateful to my husband, Carl Andrew Stambaugh, for being the most patient partner and best paddling buddy ever. Thank you for filling our life together with love, laughter, and adventure.

Thank you to my aunt and uncle, Bev and Dave Braun, for accompanying me on many trips for this book, even though you asked for it by taking me on all those camping trips as a child...

Thanks, too, to my editors, Katie Benoit Cardoso and Evan Helmlinger. It was because of their continued patience and unflagging support that this book came together—finally.

Thank you to everyone at FalconGuides for giving me the opportunity to share my passion for exploring the Commonwealth of Kentucky with readers of this book in an effort to help them do it as well!

I hope this guide inspires readers to get out and explore the woodlands and waterways of this great state and then work to preserve and create additional public access so future generations can behold the wonders too.

Happy trails.

—Carrie "Mudfoot" Stambaugh

Introduction

The Commonwealth of Kentucky boasts more miles of shoreline than any other US state with the exception of Alaska, according to a compilation of miles by C. M. Dupier Jr., a professor of geology and anthropology at Cumberland College. In all, it is estimated that the state has more than 1,500 square miles of navigable water surface area spread out over more than 13,000 miles of natural rivers, streams, and the state's fifty man-made reservoirs. But that's just a sliver of the estimated 90,000 miles of waterways that comprise the twelve hydraulic basins draining the Commonwealth of Kentucky.

The eastern half of the state can receive on average 46 inches of rain annually. In recent years, there have been many record rain events as climate change increasingly brings warmer temperatures and flooding rains. Of the water that falls on the Bluegrass State, more than half of it evaporates, making the climate similar to that of the South American cities of Rio De Janeiro, Brazil, and Buenos Aires, Argentina.

Kentucky is shaped by its karst geology, defined by a landscape underlain by dissolvable limestone rock. The massive underground plumbing system allows much of the rainfall water to drain from the surface and flow through miles of underground streams. Some of the most striking landscape features are created from the force of moving water. Kentucky's most famous and signature industry, bourbon, is also defined by the mineral-laden waters springs, rivers, and underground aquifers that are used in the distillation of the spirit.

All this water flows through a network of streams and rivers across the Commonwealth, with most of it making its way into the mighty Ohio and Mississippi Rivers. There are some fifty rivers in Kentucky, along with hundreds of streams, creeks, licks, branches, springs, runs, drains, or whatever other colorful colloquialisms the residents in that particular hollow named them.

Along the way, much of this water also spends time impounded in a flood control lake. Largely built and managed by the US Army Corps of Engineers, Kentucky's network of reservoirs is the result of annual flood control legislation that began in the 1930s. The easternmost lakes of Dewey, Yatesville, Paintsville, and Grayson are little more than flooded, narrow mountain river valleys. During the fall and winter, the lakes drop down to little more than muddy streams. Reservoirs in the south and westernmost part of the state—notably Lake Cumberland, Kentucky Lake, and Lake Barkley—are massive impounds of water. Kentucky Lake is the largest man-made reservoir in the eastern United States. In addition to providing a commercial fishery and a popular recreation asset, Kentucky Lake is a part of the intercontinental waterway. Sailboat races and large commercial barges ferry international trade through these areas. The United States moves more than 640 million tons of commodity freight annually using inland waterways that include Kentucky's.

Humans have been plying the waters of Kentucky for thousands of years. From the ancient Native American peoples to modern Kentuckians, the natural features have provided a source of transportation, drinking water, food, and environmental splendor.

Beginning as early as the 1600s, settlers began traveling the rivers here, first in canoes, then later on larger log rafts, before transitioning to the mighty steamboats and, finally, today's plethora of petroleum-powered crafts.

The Ohio River long served as a boundary between northern and southern Indian tribes who used Kentucky as their hunting grounds, which have been chronicled by Kentucky's historian laureate Dr. Thomas D. Clark. The Ohio River is the nations' second-largest river, behind only the Mississippi. The Ohio River begins in Pittsburgh, Pennsylvania, at the confluence of the Monongahela and Allegheny Rivers and flows into the Mississippi River at the town of Barlow Bottom, Kentucky.

Along the 665-mile stretch of the Ohio River from the mouth of the Big Sandy River at Catlettsburg to its confluence with the Mississippi River at Barlow Bottoms, commerce moves up and down through the series of navigational locks and dams maintained by the federal government.

Between Charleston, West Virginia, and the community of Lloyd in Greenup County lays one of the country's busiest inland ports. Just beyond this hub is one of the most breathtaking and historic waterways in the country, the Ohio River Valley, through which thousands of early Americans floated on their way to lives all across the interior of the country.

Paddling today is an excellent way to see, experience, and understand Kentucky's geology, history, and culture. There are hundreds of public access points in rivers, lakes, and streams across the Commonwealth, with more being added almost every year as the public increasingly turns back to its natural features for recreation and the promotion of tourism. This is particularly true in rural, mountainous parts of the state where the coal economy has severely declined and residents look to boost tourism. The use of human-powered watercraft has soared in popularity on Kentucky waterways in recent years as well, providing an important economic development opportunity for many rural Kentucky communities hit hard by economic decline.

Kentucky's waterways are managed by a variety of different governmental agencies, including the Kentucky Department of Fish and Wildlife, the US Army Corps of Engineers, Kentucky State Parks, the Office of Kentucky State Nature Preserves, the National Park Service, and the US Forest Service. In addition, Kentucky waterways are overseen by citizen-led organizations interested in issues that range from recreational boat access to water quality. The largest and most prominent citizen-led organization is the Kentucky Waterways Alliance, which was founded in 1993.

Section 151.100 of Kentucky's Revised Statutes defines public waterways as follows: "Water occurring in any stream, lake, ground water, subterranean water, or other body of water in the Commonwealth which may be applied to any useful and beneficial purpose is hereby declared to be a natural resource and public water of

Whether by canoe or kayak Kentucky is a great place to explore by paddle. CARRIE STAMBAUGH

Hidden waterfalls come alive along the Little Sandy after summer rains. CARRIE STAMBAUGH

the Commonwealth and subject to control or regulation for the public welfare as provided in KRS Chapters 146, 149, 151, 262, and 350.029 and 433.750 to 433.757."

The right to public access of the waterways has largely been guaranteed in Kentucky. Like many states, courts have held that landowners own to the middle or "thread" of a waterway, but the public's right to navigate those waterways has superseded the property owners. In 1985, a court ruling determined that right extends to recreation including boating, fishing, and swimming. The issue of what qualifies as "navigable" in Kentucky has historically also been quite broad because of the states long history of using even some relatively small waterways as means of transporting goods. However, according to an American Whitewater analysis, the law does not consider small waterways as "navigable in fact" if they are only "sufficient to allow pleasure boaters, hunters, or fisherman to float their skiffs or canoes," therefore effectively blocking public access—and, in many cases, public protection—to hundreds of small streams. A non-navigable stream is the private property of the individual landowner.

Nine Kentucky rivers are designated as "wild rivers." This designation encompasses 114 miles of waterways and 26,000 acres. The Kentucky Wild Rivers Act of 1972 protects the rights-of-way from construction and many other man-made intrusions. Wild Rivers are just that—clean, free-flowing, and scenic.

These waterways are among the most scenic in the eastern Appalachian Mountains and are portions of Bad Branch, Red River, Rockcastle, Rock Creek, Cumberland, Martins Fork of the Cumberland, Little Fork of the Cumberland, Big South Fork of the Cumberland, and the Green River. Only the Red River is designated a federal wild and scenic river.

Eastern Kentucky

1 Tygarts Creek

This paddle is a 12.6-mile float on Tygarts Creek, which starts in Olive Hill, a Kentucky trail town. It features a 6.5-mile gorge section, including the geological feature known as the Devil's Backbone. The paddle ends at the entrance to Carter Caves State Resort Park. The creek is windy and passes under numerous rocky overhangs, some which stretch almost the entire width of the creek!

County: Carter
Start: Olive Hill Depot Boat Ramp at Ky. 986
N38 17.974', W83 10.461'
End: Carter Caves Boat Ramp at Ky. 182
N38 20.311', W83 07.413'
Length: 12.6 miles
Float Time: 6 hours
Difficulty Rating: Easy to Moderate
Rapids: I, II-1
River Type: Rocky, mountain stream
Current: moderate to swift
River Gradient: 5 feet per mile
River Gauge: USGS 03217000 Tygarts Creek
at Greenup, KY.

Water levels below 150 cfs make this paddle tough to complete in a day. The best paddling is when the river is flowing at 300 cfs or above.

Land Status: Mostly private
Boats Used: Canoe, Kayak, SUP
Season: Spring and fall
Fees or Permits: No
Nearest City/Town: Olive Hill
Maps: USGS Olive Hill, Grahn
Organizations: Carter Caves State Resort Park, 344 Caveland Dr., Olive Hill, KY 41164; (606) 286-4411, parks.ky.gov/parks/resortparks/carter-caves
Contacts/Outfitters: Dragonfly Outdoor Adventures, 52B Treasure Cove Road, Greenup, KY 41144; (606) 465-0306; dragonflyoutdooradventures.com

Estep's Outdoor Kayak and Canoe Rentals, 4609 South State Hwy 7, Grayson, KY 41143, (606) 474-7539 (formerly Prichard's).

Getting There

To Shuttle Point/Take-out: The take-out is at the KY 182 Bridge at Carter Caves State Resort Park. To reach the take-out, take I-64 to exit 161 U.S. 60. Follow U.S. 60 north out of Olive Hill for 1.2 miles then turn left on KY 182. Follow it for 2.5 miles.

The parking area lies on the right just before you reach the bridge and entrance to the park.

To Put-in from Take-out: Turn right onto Ky. 182. Follow it for 2.5 miles to the intersection with U.S. 60. Turn left and follow it 5.2 miles, crossing under I-64 at mile 1.2. After another 4 miles, turn left on to Ky. 986. In one-tenth of a mile, take a right to the put-in on Tygart Street.

The paddle begins at the Olive Hill Depot Trailhead and Campground. Access is at Tygart Street, just before the Ky. 986 Bridge. A sign designates the access point.

River Overview

Tygarts Creek flows through one of the most spectacular river gorges in Kentucky. Created by water flowing through its porous limestone bedrock over the millennia, Tygarts Creek features mild rapids and soaring gray bluffs rising from the water's edge along with many overhanging rocks. The creek flows over a rock, gravel, and mud bottom. Hardwood forests top the bluffs and surround the creek to the bank in most areas. A tributary of the Ohio River, the river flows 88 miles through Carter County and Greenup County. It was named after Michael Tygart, a contemporary of Daniel Boone, who "discovered" the creek, settled the area, and later drowned in the creek near its mouth in Greenup County.

Tygarts Creek has many undercut cliff sides that create small, sheltered coves. CARRIE STAMBAUGH

The Paddle

The paddle begins at the Olive Hill Depot Trailhead. There is plenty of parking, but this is also the trailhead for popular horse trails and the site of campouts. The bank here is about 12 feet high and grassy, so it can become slick in wet weather.

Immediately after putting in, the creek goes under the Ky. 986 Bridge, and then at mile 0.25, the water intake for the city of Olive Hill crosses the river. In low water levels, it is not possible to paddle over it; portage can be made on either side of the river. At mile 0.75, a rock shelf extends across the river; at lower water levels, this might require some dragging, but at 200 cfs, we were able to slide right over it. At mile 1.75, the first rock walls come into view, rising about 30 feet on river right. At mile 1.9, the creek flows under an overhang of rock for a quarter-mile, which extends almost the width of the creek—about 20 feet in this section.

CARTER CAVES STATE RESORT PARK

Carter Caves State Resort Park is one of Kentucky's true public gems. In addition to its namesake caves, there are seven natural arches in the park, accessible via more than 30 miles of hiking trails. The largest natural bridge in the state of Kentucky, Smokey Bridge, is located within the park, and the Carter Caves Natural Bridge is the only arch in the state with a paved roadway on top!

The parks caves are a main attraction, with tours offered year-round in Cascade and X Caves. Cascade Cave, one of the largest of Carter County's 200-plus caves, features a 30-foot underground waterfall and a reflecting pond. Tours of X Cave show off its unique underground formations. Saltpetre Cave near the visitor's center was used to produce gunpowder during the War of 1812. Simon Kenton visited the cave and near its entrance carved his name with the year 1783. It is open for guided tours only.

A climbing and rappelling area was designated within the park recently, and on occasion, the park offers ziplining. During its annual Winter Adventure Weekend, dozens of additional cave tours, workshops, organized hikes, paddles, and more take place. It is usually held on the third weekend of January. Visit winteradventureweekend.com for more information and a schedule of events.

Carter Caves State Resort Park features a lodge, campground and cottages, restaurant, miniature golf, tennis courts, and a swimming pool. Visitors can also fish or paddle on the 45-acre Smokey Valley Lake. Horseback riding is also available. The park offers a full slate of cultural events throughout the year, including a Pioneer Weekend complete with historical reenactors.

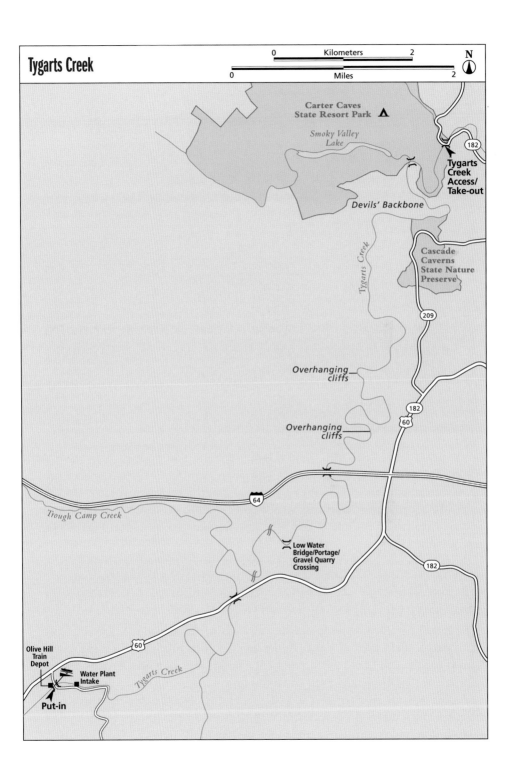

Tygarts Creek

Carter Caves
State Resort Park Λ

Smoky Valley
Lake

182

Tygarts
Creek
Access/
Take-out

Devils' Backbone

Cascade
Caverns
State Nature
Preserve

Tygarts Creek

209

Overhanging
cliffs

182

60

Overhanging
cliffs

64

Trough Camp Creek

Low Water
Bridge/Portage/
Gravel Quarry
Crossing

182

60

Olive Hill
Train
Depot

Water Plant
Intake

Tygarts Creek

Put-in

N

0   Kilometers   2

0   Miles   2

Undercut rocks make for stunning scenery along Tygarts Creek. CARRIE STAMBAUGH

The creek is lined with hardwoods and topped with hemlock and other ever-greens throughout this section, although some homes and farms are visible. During my paddle in early April, the banks were colored with bluebells, white trillium, and blooming redbuds. Deer and waterfowl, including blue heron and mallard ducks, were plentiful.

At mile 3.3, the creek crosses under a concrete bridge, just past the remnants of an older bridge. A second bridge, which carries U.S. 60 over the creek, is at mile 3.5. After a large S curve, the first significant rapid, a mild Class II, is at mile 4.9. The rapid contains a nice wave train.

At mile 5.2 is a low water bridge that serves as an access road to a gravel quarry. I have seen paddlers in small kayaks go through the metal tubing. Not a smart move. A smart paddler will take-out and portage the bridge on either side. Beware of large dump trucks that frequently speed down this road.

At mile 6.8, the river narrows and passes under the twin bridges that carry I-64 above it. Some paddlers like to access the river between the two bridges, but it requires a 100-yard steep descent after exiting to the median of the freeway.

Almost immediately after passing under the bridge, you enter the gorge section of the paddle. Rock walls soar over 60 feet on either side of the river, and at mile 7.9, a large undercut rock stretches above the entire width of the river once again. It contains several individual coves, which can be explored and have ceilings of about 30 feet.

At mile 9.5, another small tributary enters the river on the left from a natural tunnel, just before a sharp S curve in the river. The tunnel, one of the largest in the state of Kentucky, is on private property and can only be seen from the river during late fall and early spring. Watch for paddles organized by Carter Caves State Park for a chance to explore the tunnel. The river makes another sharp curve as it passes around the Devil's Backbone.

After crossing under a small wooden bridge and a sign denoting the boundary of the State Park, the take-out is on river left just before the bridge at mile 12.6.

2 Grayson Lake

This is an easy loop paddle on Grayson Lake in the Clifty Creek area that leads to a hidden waterfall. It has become one of the most popular paddles in the area and can, therefore, be quite crowded on weekends. The paddle is just off the main lake. Very close to the main channel of the Clifty Creek area, paddlers pass through a shallow cove where the waterway narrows to a few feet across as it passes a short distance under a very low rock overhang before opening up to a pool under high cliff walls at the bottom of a multi-tiered waterfall.

Counties: Carter, Elliott
Start and End: Clifty Creek Boat Ramp
N 38 13.806', W83 24.630'
Length: 5 miles
Float Time: 2.5 hours
Difficulty Rating: Easy
Rapids: None
River Type: Lake
River Gradient: none
River Gauge: Lake level can be found at www .lrh-wc.usace.army.mil/wm/?basin/lsa/grl
Land Status: Public
Nearest City/Town: Grayson
Boats Used: Canoe, kayak, SUP
Season: Spring, summer, fall; this paddle is not accessible when the lake is at its winter pool of 637 feet.
Fees or Permits: None

Maps: USGS Bruin
Organizations: US Army Corps of Engineers Huntington District; Resource Manager can be reached at (606) 474-5107 or (606) 474-5815. US Army Corps of Engineers, Grayson Lake, 50 Launch Ramp Road, Grayson, KY 41143. www.lrh.usace.army.mil/missions/civil-works/recreation/kentucky/grayson-lake. Grayson Lake State Park, 314 Grayson Lake State Park Rd., Olive Hill, KY 41164, (606) 474-9727
Contacts/Outfitters: Dragonfly Outdoor Adventures, 52B Treasure Cove Rd., Greenup, KY 41144; (606) 465-0306; dragonflyoutdoor adventures.com
    Estep's Outdoor Kayak and Canoe Rentals, 4609 South State Hwy 7, Grayson, KY 41143, (606) 474-7539 (formerly Prichard's).

Getting There

To Put-in/Take-out: From I-64, exit at Grayson (#172). Follow Ky. 7 south for 9.5 miles to a gravel road on the right just before a bridge (2.1 miles past the dam and main marina).

River Overview

Grayson Lake was created by the impoundment of the Little Sandy River between Sandy Hook and Grayson to control floodwaters. The river itself forms in southern Elliott County and flows 85.4 miles through Elliott, Carter, and Greenup Counties before entering the Ohio River at Greenup in northeast Kentucky.

Known as the grotto falls of Clifty Creek, this cascade is hidden from the main lake.
CARRIE STAMBAUGH

The Army Corps of Engineers built the earth- and rock-filled dam to create Grayson Lake in 1964. At seasonal pool, the lake covers more than 1,500 acres and boasts sandstone walls as high as 150 feet along its 74-mile shoreline. The lake is popular with anglers and motorized watercraft, but it does feature a number of zones designated as no-wake.

The Paddle

This paddle starts at the popular Clifty Creek boat ramp, so use caution when parking and unloading at the location. This is a popular spot for swimming and fishing. From the ramp, turn right or east, following the main channel of the Clifty Creek branch of Grayson Lake. The banks here are moderately sloped and rocky with thick tree cover along most of the banks. As the lake curves south at mile 0.3, the first set of high sandstone cliffs come into view on the northern and western side of the lake.

At mile 0.5, a good spot to anchor for a swim is at the point of a horseshoe curve on river right. There is a sign here warning boaters of shallow rocks; there is, in fact, a ledge of rock just a foot or two beneath the surface, creating a nice platform that is an excellent spot to anchor for a swim. Across the lake is the popular Neyers' Cove area, named for a local Olympic diver Megan Neyer who reportedly would practice diving from the steep cliffs here, which are accessible from Ky. 896.

Cliff jumping is now strictly prohibited at Grayson Lake, and violators can be fined up to $5,000 by authorities, who frequently patrol the lake during the busy summer season. Drowning caused by injuries sustained when jumping or diving from cliffs is an all too common occurrence on Grayson Lake, with an average of one death every couple of years.

Continue paddling west, passing between steep, wooded hills on a relatively straight stretch of lake. In the summer, the hillside homes above the lake on the southern or river right bank are invisible from the water, although traffic noise and the occasional crowing rooster can be heard.

After one mile, the lakes begin to wind gently. This area features many large cliffs along the northern bank, and swallows are frequently seen. In wet weather, the Luke Carroll Branch may create a small waterfall on river right at mile 1.5. At mile 1.6, the main channel of the lake appears to flow northward toward the Sam Carroll Branch. Follow the channel a short distance to another waterfall here where the branch enters the lake at mile 1.9. When the lake is at regular summer pool, a gravel sandbar is located just in front of the base of the falls and is another great spot for anchoring for a swim.

Heading back, retracing your steps just as you turn the corner from the Sam Carroll Branch, bear right and paddle the back of the cove, where a small, hidden channel comes into view, at roughly the 2.2-mile mark.

This is Far Clifty Creek, and there is standing timber just below the surface, and in dry years, this area can become inaccessible and clogged in by grasses. Continue following the narrow channel until it curves sharply and flows below an overhang in

Grayson Lake

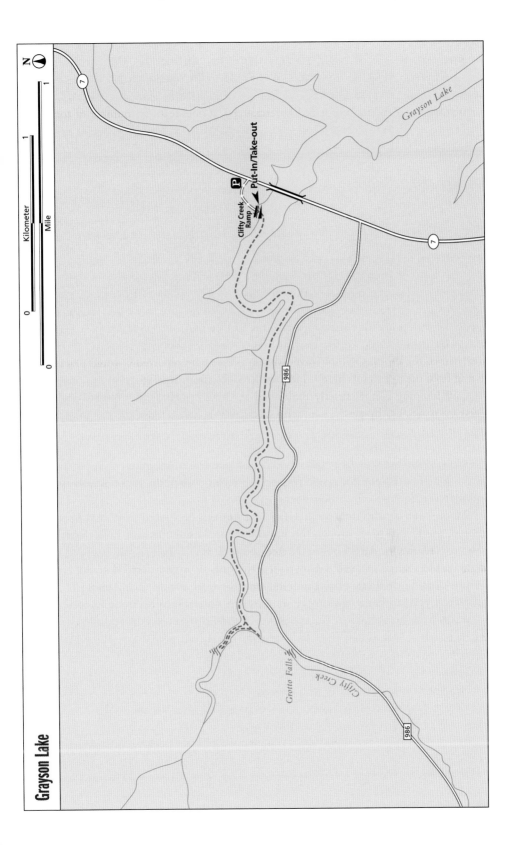

Grayson Lake features sandstone bluffs, hidden coves, and waterfalls. CARRIE STAMBAUGH

the cliffside and between large fallen boulders. Make sure to announce your entrance, as this is a popular spot with paddlers, and the path between the rocks in only wide enough to accommodate a single boat.

Upon entering this area, at mile 2.6, paddles can be tucked away and boaters should "push" their way through this narrow channel using the rock walls on either side to guide them. After about 100 feet, the rock wall curves sharply away to the right, and you enter a small but deep pool at the base of a triple-tiered waterfall as the Whitley/Far Clifty Branch flows into the creek between two steep hillsides.

When you are done gawking at the "hidden waterfall," turn around and make your way back to Clifty Boat Ramp for a total paddle of just less than 5 miles.

3 Little Sandy River

This is a paddle along a quiet and scenic section of the Little Sandy River upriver from its impoundment at Grayson Lake. The river winds its way through the rolling hills of eastern Elliott County on this stretch, passing primarily between steep undercut sandstone cliffs and through narrow river valleys. There are numerous small tributaries that make excellent small detours on this paddle when navigable, revealing a number of 50- to 60-foot wet-weather waterfalls.

County: Elliott
Start: Heritage Canoe Carrydown
N 38 07.101', W 83 06.347'
End: Newfoundland Boat Ramp
N 38 08.697', W 83 04.065'
Length: 4.6 miles
Float Time: 3 hours
Difficulty Rating: Easy
Rapids: I
River Type: Rocky, mountain stream
Current: moderate
River Gradient: 4.6 feet per mile
River Gauge: No gauge for this stretch of river
Land Status: Public/private

Nearest City/Town: Sandy Hook
Boats Used: Canoes, kayaks, SUP
Season: Spring, summer, fall
Fees or Permits: No fees or permits required.
Maps: USGS Bruin, Isonville
Organizations/Contacts/Outfitters: Dragonfly Outdoor Adventures, 52B Treasure Cove Rd., Greenup, KY 41144; (606) 465-0306; dragon flyoutdooradventures.com
  Laurel Gorge Cultural Heritage Center; (606) 738-5543
  Estep's Outdoor Kayak and Canoe Rentals, 4609 South State Hwy 7 Grayson, KY 41143, (606) 474-7539 (formerly Prichard's).

Getting There

To Shuttle Point/Take-out: From Grayson, take U.S. 7 south for 18 miles. Turn right at sign for junction of Ky. 607 and immediately turn left into gravel parking lot at the Newfoundland Boat Ramp. There is parking for approximately twenty vehicles including boat trailers and a paved put-in to the river.

To Put-In from Take-out: Continue on U.S. 7 for 2.7 miles. Turn left onto Old Laurel Curves Road, at sign for Laurel Gorge Cultural Heritage Center. After crossing a narrow bridge over the Little Sandy River, turn right. A gravel parking lot is immediately to the right. There is parking for approximately twelve vehicles and a carry down for watercraft.

River Overview

The Little Sandy River flows 85.4 miles from its headwaters in Elliott County, near the community of Sandy Hook through Elliott, Carter, and Greenup Counties before entering the Ohio River at Greenup. In the spring and fall, water levels on the river

The Little Sandy River has carved a striking sandstone gorge on its way to Grayson Lake.
CARRIE STAMBAUGH

upstream from the lake can vary daily, and since the only gauge is below the lake, water levels should be visually checked before launching.

The Paddle

This paddle begins just downriver from the mouth of the scenic Laurel Gorge, where the Laurel Creek empties into the Little Sandy River. This paddle is characterized by undercut sandstone banks and cliffs and is in a heavily wooded corridor with large hemlocks, rhododendron, and other hardwoods.

The river is narrow from 25 to 30 feet and winds its way northeast toward the lake. In the summer when Grayson Lake is at summer pool, there is little to no current on the river and many small tributaries are accessible. In the spring and fall, when water levels are lower, the paddling is nice, but deadfalls can sometimes block navigation.

The river heads almost directly north during the first section of paddle passing almost immediately between high sandstone cliffs during its first half mile before it turns east away from the nearby Laurel Curves Road, making a sharp S curve

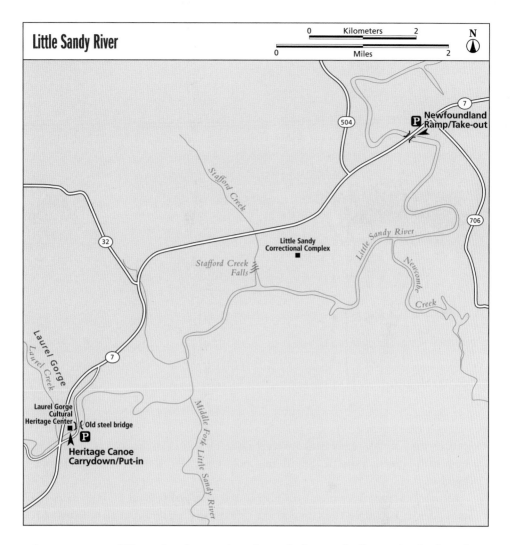

between steep cliffs turning first south and west before gradually turning back to the northeast.

At mile 1, a small tributary descends over a steep cliff forming a small waterfall on river right (south). A short distance later, the Middle Fork of the Little Sandy enters from the south at mile 1.1, and the river gradually turns to the north, passing another small waterfall on the right and straightens out for a stretch. At mile 1.3, another tributary enters from river left (west), and at mile 1.4, the river turns again to the east, beneath a scenic rock outcropping and another small waterfall enters the river on river right.

At mile 2.0, Stafford Creek enters from the north, also creating a small waterfall. High above the river is the Little Sandy Correctional Complex, invisible from the

Undercut rocks along the Little Sandy are a great place to explore when the water is calm.
CARRIE STAMBAUGH

river during most of the year. At mile 2.5, a small tributary enters from the right, creating a nice sandbar. At mile 3.0, Newcombe Creek enters the river from the south, creating a wide sandy bank on river right. The north of the river is lined with a high cliff. This is a popular local fishing hole, especially in the spring during the white bass run.

At mile 3.5, the river enters a U-turn to the west and is lined on both sides by high undercut sandstone cliffs topped with rhododendron and mountain laurel. At mile 4, the river curves again, heading north and east, before curving back to the west at mile 4.4. Rosewood Creek enters the river here from the east.

The take-out is to the right at mile 4.6, just below the Ky. 7 Bridge on river right. There is a steep concrete ramp.

4 Blaine's Creek / Yatesville Lake

This is an out-and-back loop paddle on the quieter southern section of the lake near its headwaters. The paddle can be enlarged easily into a long day trip or multiday camping trip. This paddle is outside the Yatesville Lake State Park area, but the shoreline is all public land, most of it part of the 13,191-acre Yatesville Lake Wildlife Management Area.

County: Lawrence

Start and End: Rich Creek Ramp
N 38 08.697', W 83 04.065'

Length: 3.5 miles

Float Time: 2.5 hours

Difficulty Rating: Easy

Rapids: None

River Type: Lake

Current: Slow

River Gradient: 1.0

River Gauge: Current information on lake levels can be found at: www.lrh-wc.usace.army.mil/wm/?basin/bsa/ybc

Land Status: Public

Nearest City/Town: Louisa

Boats Used: Canoe, Kayak, SUP

Season: Spring, summer, fall. When lake levels fall to winter pool, the lake is no longer accessible from this boat ramp.

Fees or Permits: No permits or fees required

Maps: USGS Blaine, Adams

Organizations/Contacts/Outfitters: US Army Corps of Engineers, 708 Yatesville Dam Road, Louisa, KY 41230. The US Army Corps of Engineers Resource Manager can be reached at (606) 686-2412.

Yatesville Lake State Park, 2667 Pleasant Ridge Road, Louisa, KY 41230, (606) 673-1492.

Legend Outfitters, 606 Beach Road, Louisa, KY 41230, (606) 615-4778, www.Legend Outfitters.org.

Getting There

To Put-in/Take-out: At the intersection of U.S. 23 and Ky. 32 in Louisa, take Ky. 32 west for 9.3 miles. The Rich Creek Boat Ramp and parking lot is on the right just before crossing the creek.

River Overview

Just approaching 30 years old, Yatesville Lake was created by damming Blaine's Creek, a tributary of the Big Sandy River. Work began on its earthen dam in 1988, and the lake officially opened in 1992. It is a narrow, winding waterway covering approximately 3.5 square miles and has the capacity to hold in excess of 83,300 acre-feet of water.

The US Army Corps of Engineers says the "boatable miles" upstream from the dam is 20.6 miles. Downstream of its tailwaters, there is an additional 18.1 miles of water before its confluence with the Big Sandy River. Yatesville has become one of the best lakes in the state for largemouth bass fishing and, therefore, hosts many

Yatesville Lake's rocky shoreline can create navigational hazards for motorboats but not the paddled craft. CARRIE STAMBAUGH

fishing tournaments—sometimes with hundreds of boats descending on the waterway at the same time. Bluegill and crappie are also plentiful, along with catfish.

Yatesville Lake State Park is located at the northwestern end of the lake and contains a campground, marina, and golf course. There are boat-in only campsites in the park, making this a possible canoe-camping destination.

The Paddle

This paddle explores the remote southern end of the lake, which is much quieter than the portion of the lake near the dam and Yatesville Lake State Resort Park. The land surrounding the lake is hilly, with some ridges topping out at near 1,000 feet of elevation. In contrast, the lake has a surface elevation of 630 feet at summer pool. The steep hills are covered in hardwood forest, although there are some fairly broad bottomland and significant wetland areas along the lake. There are also many coves holding tall standing timber.

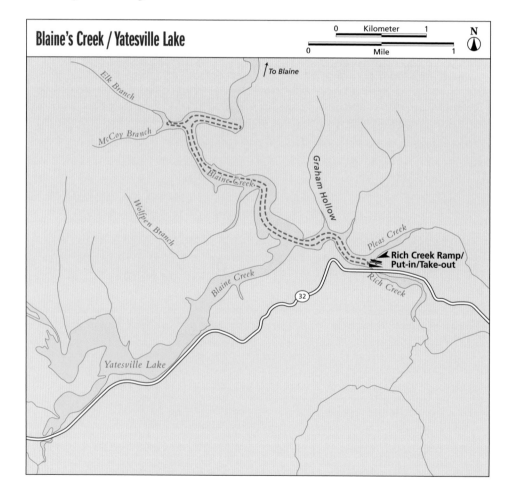

Blaine's Creek / Yatesville Lake

The lake averages 18 feet in depth but can reach 60 feet in areas. On this paddle, there is often only a small sliver of rocky shoreline, which often drops off quickly into deep water. Finding a place to land can be tricky.

From the put-in, stay to river right (west) to head toward the main channel of the lake, passing a few small coves along the way. The first to the right is where Pleas Creek enters the lake. At 0.6 mile, you will reach the main channel. This is the widest point of the lake on your paddle—measuring close to 900 feet wide, or nearly 0.2 mile. Stay along the river right shore as the river turns to head north toward the downriver bulk of the lake. (A left-hand turn will take you south toward the Irish Creek area of the lake.)

There is a gently sloping grassy bottom at a point where the Rich Creek arm of the lake meets the main channel. This is inhabited by a flock of Canada geese, who can get pretty upset if you attempt to land here. The bank is lined in this area with pink and red flowering rosemallow, which is a native hibiscus.

At mile 1.1, you reach the cove on the western shore (river left) where Wolfpen Branch enters the lake. This cove features standing timber; watch out for the stands that can be just below the surface. This is an excellent area to make some fishing casts, since bass love to use the trees for cover.

Continue heading north, and at mile 1.7, to the west is the entrance to a large cove where McCoy Branch and Elk Branch enter the lake. The cove is just as the lake enters a sharp turn to the east. Again, this is an excellent spot to float and cast.

This spot serves as the turn around on this paddle. As you head back to the put-in, be careful crossing the channel in this curve, as motorized craft frequent the area.

5   Levisa Fork of the Big Sandy River

This is a nice float for beginners and families. The river is between 80 and 110 feet wide as it winds its way north between deep, muddy banks, which are heavily wooded with mature trees. The water often runs clear but can become muddy after rains.

Homes and farms are located all along the waterway, but it is quiet and serene with only occasional noise from a passing train, vehicle, or the laughter and talking from residents who live along the river.

County: Johnson
Start: Paintsville River Access Boat Ramp on Chessie Lane
N 37 48.853', W 82 47.494'
End: Tim Price Landing, Offutt, KY
N 37 51.141', W 82 43.864'
Length: 7.5 miles
Float Time: 3 hours
Difficulty: Easy
Rapids: I
River Type: Rocky mountain stream
Current: Moderate
River Gradient: 1 foot per mile

River Gauge: USGS 03212500 Levisa Fork at Paintsville. The minimum reading should be 400 cfs.
Land Status: Private
Nearest City/Town: Paintsville
Boats Used: Canoe, Kayak, SUP
Season: Any
Fees or Permits: No fees or permits required
Maps: USGS Paintsville, Offutt
Organizations: Paintsville/Johnson County Trail Town on Facebook
Contacts/Outfitters: Legend Outfitters, 606 Beach Rd., Louisa, KY 41230, (606) 615-4778, www.LegendOutfitters.org

Getting There

To Shuttle Point/Take-out: From U.S. 23, U.S. 460 (The Mountain Parkway), and Ky. 40 in Staffordsville: Take Ky. 40 east for 0.5 mile, then turn right onto U.S. 23 Business route. Follow it for 1.6 miles. Then turn left onto Third Street; after 0.4 miles, it makes a turn to the right and becomes Margaret Heights/Ky. 40, then Euclid Avenue/Ky. 40. Continue on the road for another 0.6 mile then turn left onto Ky. 581. Follow it for 7 miles. Then turn left onto Wiley Branch Road, and in 0.1 mile, turn right onto Branch Road, crossing the river. Then turn right onto Ky. 2040 and then left onto County Road 3224. Tim Price Landing is located on private property. Close all gates after crossing through.

To Put-in from Take-out: Turn left onto Ky. 2040, following it for 1 mile. Then turn left onto Branch Road, crossing the Levisa. At the end of the bridge, make a left turn onto Wiley Branch Road, then turn right onto Ky. 581 after 0.2 mile. Follow Ky. 581 (Tudor Key Road) for approximately 7 miles. Then turn right onto Ky. 40 (Euclid Avenue) after 0.2 mile, turn left onto Depot Street, in 0.2 miles, turn left onto State Street. In 0.1 mile, turn left onto Chessie Lane. Follow Chessie Lane for 0.1 mile

The Levisa Fork of the Big Sandy River was called Chatterwa by Native Americans, a name local trail advocates are hoping to revive. CARRIE STAMBAUGH

to its intersection with River Road. The parking lot and boat ramp are located near the intersection at the mouth of Paint Creek.

River Overview

The Levisa Fork of the Big Sandy River is one of the largest watersheds in eastern Kentucky.

Chatterwa is the Native American name for the river, which flows from Virginia into Pike County, where it is immediately impounded to form Fishtrap Lake. After leaving Pike County, it flows through Floyd, Johnson, and Lawrence counties, where it joins the Tug Fork at Louisa, Kentucky/Fort Gay, West Virginia to become the Big Sandy River. Three additional flood control lakes are located along the river's watershed: Paintsville Lake, Dewey Lake, and Yatesville Lake. The river can still rise and fall tens of feet very quickly following heavy rains. Be sure to check water conditions and pay attention to storms upstream.

The Levisa Fork was rerouted at Pikeville in one of the world's largest civil engineering projects in the western hemisphere, known as the Pikeville Cut-Through. The river made a tight, horseshoe-like loop around the foot of Peach Orchard Mountain, inside of which the City of Pikeville grew. The sharp turn was prone to devastating flooding. More than twenty local, state, and federal agencies were involved in the project, which took place between 1973 and 1987. In all, a total of 18 million cubic yards of dirt were moved, creating a 1,300-foot-wide, 3,700-foot-long, and

DAWKINS LINE RAIL TRAIL

Kentucky's longest and newest rail trail, the Dawkins Line Rail Trail is an 18-mile-long multi-use trail that begins in Hagerhill and ends in Royalton. The trail crosses through Johnson and Magoffin Counties and opened in 2013. It features twenty-four trestles that cross the numerous creeks and runs of the region, but the highlight is the 662-foot-long Gun Creek Tunnel. The linear Dawkins Line Rail Trail is part of the Kentucky State Park system.

Construction on an additional 18 miles of rail trail has long been delayed, but when completed the trail will stretch 36 miles to Evanston in Breathitt County. A second tunnel, the Tip Top Tunnel, also known as the Carver Tunnel, is 1,555 feet long and an additional ten trestles, a coal tipple, and a remote stretch of woods will be the highlights of this section.

The trail occupies what was once a railroad corridor for transporting timber from the region. The Dawkins Lumber Company constructed the first stretch of rail line beginning in 1912. Later, the C&O Railroad acquired the line and expanded it, constructing the Tip Top/Carver Tunnel until 1949. The line later became part of CSX Railroad, and it was sold to R. J. Corman. Corman filed to abandon and "railbank" the line in 2004.

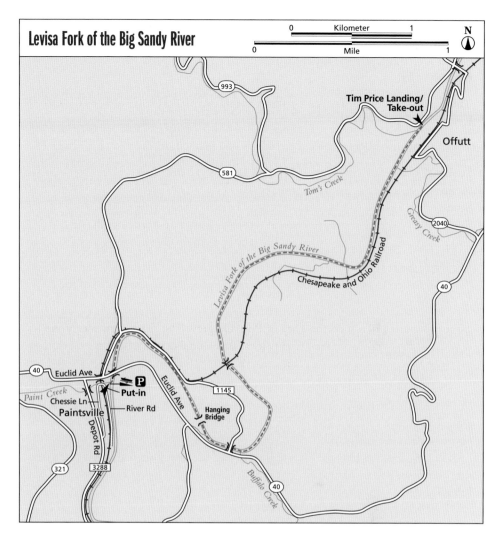

993

Tim Price Landing/
Take-out

Offutt

581

Tom's Creek

Greasy Creek

2040

Levisa Fork of the Big Sandy River

Chesapeake and Ohio Railroad

40

40 Euclid Ave

Paint Creek

Chessie Ln

Paintsville

Put-in

River Rd

Euclid Ave

1145

Hanging
Bridge

Depot Rd

321   3288

Buffalo Creek

40

523-foot-deep cut in Peach Orchard Mountain through which the Levisa Fork, a four-lane highway, and a railroad now pass. Only the Panama Canal moved more dirt.

The Paddle

This paddle begins more than 50 miles downstream of the Pikeville Cut-Through in the community of Paintsville in Johnson County, at the confluence of Paint Creek and the Levisa Fork.

The boat ramp is just upstream from a bridge carrying Euclid Avenue/Ky. 40 over the river. Almost immediately after crossing under the bridge, the river begins its approach to a horseshoe bend to the east. Big boulders line the riverbank on river left, and in low levels, there is a bumpy shoal here. Exposed rock is visible above the tree line along ridge tops throughout the paddle in all seasons.

In addition to dozens of swallows darting about, I spotted a Kingfisher and several Great Blue Herons on my paddle in late June. A river otter swam along the shoreline too for several hundred yards before disappearing under a log at the mouth of a small tributary.

The fishing is also excellent along the river with populations of largemouth, smallmouth, rock, and spotted bass, along with sunfish and catfish.

At mile 1.8, cross under a hanging bridge and look up to catch another view of rocky mountainside, created for the roadway and railroad. At mile 2.3, the bridge for County Road 1145 crosses overhead. Rocky shoals can be found on either side of the river here in low water levels, so stick to the center of the stream for smooth paddling.

At mile 3.7, you pass beneath a railroad trestle. This marks the community of Thelma. Large boulders and rocks continue to dominate the banks, and a rocky shoal at mile 4.25 makes the paddle interesting.

At mile 5.25, stay left to go around a large gravel island in the middle of the river. At mile 6, the river curves to the west (river left) beneath a high ridge; the inside of the bend has collected some trash and is rocky. Again, stay to the center of the river to avoid dragging or scraping.

At mile 7.25, you pass beneath a set of power lines just before the river bends to the right again. At mile 7.6, a bright red barn and corn crib come into view on river right. This is your landmark for the take-out. The concrete boat ramp is located just past them on river right.

This is Tim Price Landing, on private property in the small community of Offutt. Mr. Price built the launch with the hope of attracting paddlers to use it and has added a small, primitive campground on his riverside farm. (Don't be alarmed if you see a cow or two at the take-out.)

The day of my paddle, the local trail town organization hosted an organized river run, and there was live bluegrass music and a bean supper upon our arrival at Tim Price Landing.

6 Johns Creek / Dewey Lake

This is a loop paddle on Johns Creek and its tributary, Copperas Creek, which form man-made Dewey Lake. When the lake is at summer pool this paddle on the eastern-most waters of the recreation area offers a quieter alternative to the 18.5-mile-long lake, which is popular with motorized watercraft.

County: Floyd
Start and End: German Bridge Campground, 7533 Ky. Route 194, Prestonsburg, Kentucky N 37 41.088', W 82 39.180'
Length: 5.5 miles
Float Time: 4 hours
Difficulty: Easy
Rapids: none
River Type: Lake
Current: Slow
River Gradient: 1.0 foot per mile
River Gauge: Johns Creek near Meta, Kentucky; minimum reading should be 100 cfs.
Land Status: Public
Nearest City/Town: Prestonsburg
Boats Used: Canoe, Kayak, SUP

Season: Year-round
Fees or Permits: No fees or permits required
Maps: USGS Lancer
Organizations: US Army Corps of Engineers Dewey Lake, 9278 Lake Rd.,,Van Lear, KY 41265, (606) 886-6709
Dewey Lake fishing/water information line: (606) 886-6398 https://www.lrh.usace .army.mil/Missions/Civil-Works/Recreation/ Kentucky/Dewey-Lake
Contacts/Outfitters: German Bridge Camp-ground: 7533 Ky. 194, Prestonsburg, KY 41653, (606) 874-1150
Jenny Wiley Lake State Resort Park, 75 Theatre Court, Prestonsburg, KY 41653, (606) 889-1790

Getting There

To Put-in/Take-out: From I-64, take U.S. 23 south (exit 191). Travel 66 miles to Ky. 1428. Turn left to travel north. In 2.5 miles, turn right onto Ky. 194 North, travel 7.2 miles crossing the German Bridge. The parking lot for the put-in is immediately to the right after crossing the bridge.

River Overview

John's Creek begins in Pike County and flows northwest into Dewey Lake in Floyd County. The lake was formed when the US Army Corps of Engineers impounded John's Creek in 1949, as part of its integrated flood reduction efforts on the Ohio River. John's Creek is a tributary of the Levisa Fork of the Big Sandy River.

The Paddle

The paddle begins at a public boat ramp next to the German Bridge. Heading down river, the paddle passes the campground, which is popular with equestrians as the 20-mile Copperas Creek Horse Trail begins there as well. The creek is approximately

Johns Creek flows through a narrow river valley in eastern Kentucky, offering mountain views.
CARRIE STAMBAUGH

40 feet wide here and calm, nestled in a wide river valley between heavily wooded mountains. The 9,000-acre Dewey Lake Wildlife Management Area surrounds the creek, which encompasses several shallow wetland areas with native plants including cattails that are home to native animals including blue heron and turtles. The waters of Johns Creek and Dewey Lake support healthy populations of fish including bass, crappie, and muskie.

A no-wake zone comes into effect a half-mile into the paddle and stretches to mile 1.1. This area has low, muddy banks on both sides and a few private houses, and the Christian Appalachian Project's summer camp have docks along the waterway.

At mile 1.5, a set of navigational buoys mark the channel, which is helpful when the lake is at winter pool and Johns Creek is at a lower level as well. At mile 1.7, Copperas Creek enters Johns Creek from the north. The mouth of the creek is wide here—reaching almost 150 feet across—but the current is gentle. A horse trail follows the edge of the creek, and it is not uncommon to spot equestrians from the water. Copperas Creek can only be paddled for 0.3 mile each way before it narrows and becomes too shallow—adding 0.6 mile to the paddle.

At mile 2.3, reenter Johns Creek and continue paddling downstream, west toward the lake for another quarter mile, where a set of small coves on either side of the creek create a nice place to turn around.

The scenery on the return trip to the German Bridge is just as lovely as that heading out—just lush, green hills and blue sky!

The paddle concludes at mile 5.5 just before crossing under the bridge.

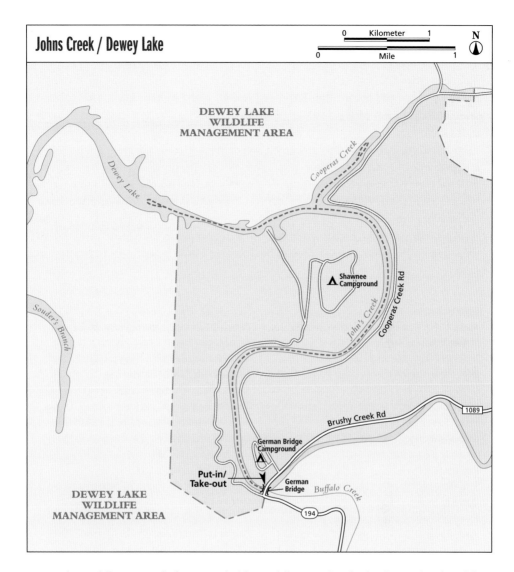

The paddle can easily be extended by paddling under the bridge and either following Johns Creek north and east along Ky. 194 North or following Buffalo Creek to the south and west along Ky. 194 South.

7 Russell Fork of the Big Sandy River

This little stretch of whitewater in the Breaks Canyon of Pine Mountain is one of the most scenic paddles in all of Kentucky. It also offers beginning and intermediate whitewater paddlers with a thrilling, beautiful float on which to practice and sharpen their skills.

It starts off with some pushy Class II waves that are easily capable of flipping an inexperienced or inattentive boater and goes all the way up to Class III+ IV whitewater at high water levels that requires some practiced self-rescue skills. In low water, this is a nice, scenic float and is popular for anglers looking to hook rainbow trout and smallmouth bass.

This is the stretch of whitewater that the Bluegrass Wildwater Association uses to train (initiate) new kayakers at their annual Spring Clinic held the first weekend in June.

County: Pike
Start: Ratliff Hole River Access (also called Potters Ford)
N 37 18.001 W 82 19.270
End: Carson Island Access
N 37 17.730', W 82 20.249'
Length: 1.1 miles
Float Time: 2 hours
Difficulty Rating: Moderate to difficult depending on water level
Rapids: III (IV)
River Type: Rocky mountain stream
Current: Swift
River Gradient: 28 feet per mile
River Gauge: USGS 03209000 Pound River below Flannagan Dam, near Haysi, VA
USGS 03208500 Russell Fork at Haysi, VA
The best water levels for this float range from 200 to 2,000 cfs on the Bartlick, Virginia, gauge on the US Army Corps of Engineers Huntington District whitewater pages at www.lrh-wc.usace.army.mil/wc/whitewater.html.

This stretch can be paddled at water levels up to 5,000 cfs, but at levels above 3,500, only experienced boaters should attempt the run.
Land Status: Public
Nearest City/Town: Elkhorn City
Boats Used: Whitewater kayak
Season: Spring, fall; after heavy rains
Fees or Permits: Yes. Parking at Ratliff Hole costs $2, the cost of a day-use pass to the Breaks Interstate Park.
Maps: USGS Elkhorn City
Organizations: Bluegrass Wildwater Association: bwa.org
AmericanWhitewater.org
Contacts/Outfitters: Breaks Interstate Park, 627 Commission Circle, Breaks, VA 24607, (276) 865-4413, www.breakspark.com
Kentucky Whitewater Rafting and Kayaking, 150 E Russell Street, Elkhorn City, KY 41522, www.kentuckywhitewater.com
Sheltowee Trace Outfitter: (800) 541-RAFT (7238) or online at www.ky-rafting.com

Getting There

From Shuttle Point (Take-out) to Put-In: The take-out is at Carson Island Access via Carson Island Road, which is just off Ky. 80, east of Elkhorn City. Follow

Carson Island Road 0.8 miles, and then turn right onto South Patty Loveless Drive Ky. 80. Follow it for 1.7 miles, and then turn right onto Breaks Park Road.

To Put-In/Take-out: The put-in is at the upper Ratliff Hole River Access, approximately 2 miles north from Elkhorn City on Ky. 80. There is lots of parking but no camping permitted, except during special events. There are a restroom and showers located here, however.

River Overview

The remote Russell Fork of the Big Sandy River passes through the Breaks Canyon, which separates Virginia and Kentucky at Pine Mountain's northern end. The 125-mile-long mountain is breached only by the Russell Fork here, which, over the millennium, has carved the deepest horseshoe-shaped gorge east of the Mississippi.

Called the "Grand Canyon of the East," the Russell Fork contains some of the most dangerous whitewater in the Southeast in its middle section. Luckily its northern and southern sections are accessible to paddlers with less than world-class paddling skills.

Preserved within 4,600-acre Breaks Interstate Park, the Russell Fork has long been off the beaten path. However, recent road improvements have expanded access, which is a good thing for the local economy, hit hard by the closure of coal mines in recent decades.

On the river, paddlers experience the steep drops and narrow passageways as the Russell Fork carves its way through the gorge, along with spectacular views of its 1,000-foot-high carved stone walls. There are also views of railroad trestles and the undulating mountains forested by hardwoods.

The Russell Fork begins in western Virginia and joins the Pound River at Bartlick, Virginia. It then flows along the border of Virginia and Kentucky through the section preserved by the Breaks Interstate Park before flowing through Pike County, Kentucky, and joining the Levisa Fork of the Big Sandy River just below Fishtrap Lake.

During its fall release season—typically four weekends in October—the middle section of the gorge attracts serious whitewater paddlers from around the world. The upper and lower sections of the river, however, offer exhilarating paddling that is accessible to paddlers with a wider range of whitewater skills and comfort.

The Paddle

This paddle is entirely within the state of Kentucky, and it includes a Class III rapid called Meatgrinder, along with a challenging Class II rapid called Pinball. These rapids should not be attempted without having mastered some basic whitewater paddling skills, including how to perform a roll, safely wet exit, and/or perform a self-rescue.

A helmet is advised. Trust me; I've done my share of swimming in this section of river while learning to whitewater kayak. I have photos of my scratched helmet, and

The Russell Fork River offers some family-friendly whitewater paddling on its upper and lower sections. CARRIE STAMBAUGH

the cuts and bruises I accumulated on one nasty swim prove this stretch of water is not to be taken lightly.

That said, this is a great paddle for beginners, as it combines the stunning scenery with live-action whitewater. The paddle begins just above what is called Ratliff Hole, also known as Potter's Ford. This stretch of river is an excellent spot to "practice" whitewater skills as both up- and downriver of the rapid are easily accessible by foot and vehicle. Skills such as rolling your kayak in live-action whitewater, how to enter and exit eddies, and how to rescue other boaters can easily be practiced all day here.

Ratliff Hole itself is located 0.25 miles downstream from the put-in used on this paddle. It is possible to put-in here as well.

Another 0.25 mile downstream is the railroad trestle where the Clinchfield Railroad crosses the Russell Fork.

From this bridge, it is less than 0.1 mile to the first rapid at mile 0.6. Meatgrinder, a Class III rapid at high water I mentioned earlier, is here. It is a series of three drops,

THE GORGE

The "middle" or "Gorge" section of the Russell Fork offers the region's most technical Class V whitewater. During the dam release season in the fall, which is usually four consecutive weekends in October, the river attracts whitewater enthusiasts from around the world.

The Gorge section of the Russell Fork is located between Garden Hole Access and Ratliff Hole (the put-in for the featured paddle). This nearly 4-mile stretch of whitewater features three Class V rapids and three big Class IV rapids. The river drops on average 140 feet per mile in this stretch, but in the horseshoe where the river carves its way around the mountain, it drops 180 feet per mile. The rapids here are characterized by narrow consecutive drops and have been described as "intensely complex, technical, violent, and continuous." This run should only be attempted by the most experienced whitewater kayakers.

During the last weekend in October is the annual Russell Fork Rendezvous. Organized by the Bluegrass Wildwater Association, the festival has been held for more than 20 years and features camping, music, food, and paddling with all proceeds benefitting American Whitewater. The highlight of the weekend for many is the Lord of the Fork Race, held on Saturday afternoon.

The Lord of the Fork Race began as a competition between friends but has since become a sanctioned event, where kayakers compete to be the first to navigate a 4-mile stretch of Class V whitewater. It is named for Jon Lord, an expert local kayaker who became pinned in a rapid and drowned in January 2004.

Russell Fork of the Big Sandy River

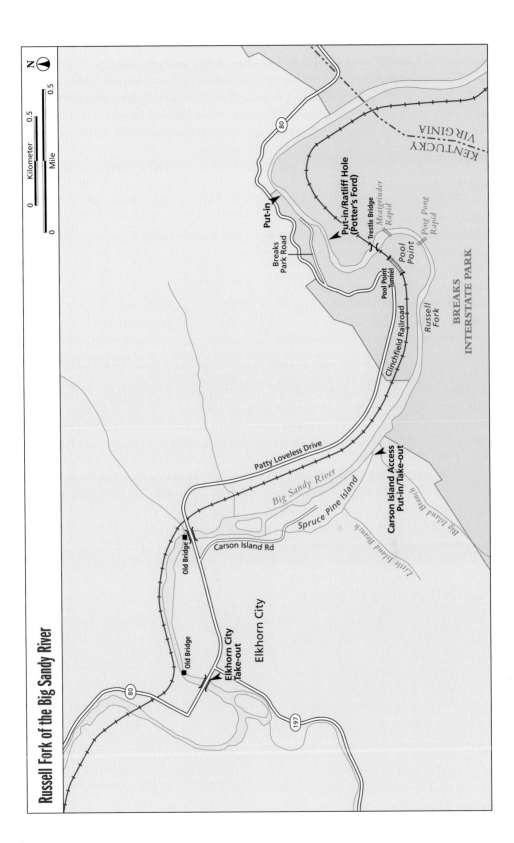

separated by hydraulics and studded with large rocks; the preferred line is to the right side of the top pour over just to the left of a boulder that splits the river in two. There is a "tongue" of water here to aim for. Get on it. From there, keep going to the second drop, aiming to hit it just left of center. The last drop is a jumble of boulders that create a hydraulic across the river; the easiest line is to the far left, but any will work as long as you aren't sideways or upside down by this point.

At the end is an eddy to the far right, which allows paddlers to gather to watch and help rescue other kayakers. There is also an eddy to the left, which is smaller and more difficult to catch but where more experienced boaters like to linger as well and again, help rescue beginners.

Another 0.1 mile later, at mile 0.7, after some nice waves of water, is the next rapid, Pinball. Pinball is a long rapid, described as a Class II or borderline Class III because it requires some maneuverability. At the top of the rapid is a pour over that presents itself with a horizon line and a large boulder splitting the current in two. The easiest line is to the right. Again, there are three distinct drops here that require skillful maneuvering. A series of eddies between rapids allow boaters to start and stop their whitewater run but can be difficult to catch in higher water levels. Catching an edge can easily flip a less experienced boater and trigger a swim through bumpy whitewater. It is often much easier to make the run all in one go.

Again, I advise from personal experience here. On my first trip through Pinball, I tried for and missed the very first eddy. Unable to roll over, I was forced to abandon my boat and "swim" the rapid. This meant I bounced on my backside with feet in the air through the second part of the rapid, which resulted in the aforementioned "proof" bruises.

The remainder of the paddle from below Pinball to the take-out at Carson Island at mile 1.1 is a pool of much calmer water but there are shallow shoals. In low and high water, this stretch can be challenging to navigate.

At moderate water levels, it is possible to paddle 1.4 miles further to Elkhorn City for a total paddle of 2.5 miles, but during low water levels, this can be a long slog.

8 Poor Fork of the Cumberland River

The Poor Fork of the Cumberland River winds through the wide river valley at the foot of Pine Mountain in Harlan County. Often paralleled by U.S. 119, or a not-so-busy-these-days rail line used primarily to haul coal from the surrounding mountains, the Poor Fork passes under two coal tipples—one active, and one retired—as well as a slew of bridges including hanging footbridges, highway bridges, and personal bridges on this stretch.

This paddle offers a glimpse at life in the Appalachian coalfields along with views of the heavily wooded hills of the nearby Ketenia State Forest to the north and, in the distance, the peak of Black Mountain, Kentucky's highest at 4,145 feet.

County: Harlan
Start: Morris Bottom Road
N 36 57.886', W 38 03.180'
End: Harlan County Shrine Park
N 36 54.720', W 83 12.237'
Length: 11 miles
Float Time: 3.5 hours
Difficulty: Easy
Rapids: I, II
River Type: Rocky, mountain stream
Current: Moderate
River Gradient: 10 feet per mile
River Gauge: USGS Poor Fork of the Cumberland at Cumberland. Minimum is 4 feet, or 130 cfs.

Land Status: Private
Nearest City/Town: Harlan
Boats Used: Kayak
Season: Spring, after heavy rains
Fees or Permits: No; however, the Shriner's Park is open to the public from dawn until dusk only.
Maps: USGS Nolansburg, Louellen
Organizations/Contacts/Outfitters: Harlan County Campground and Cabin Rentals, 8331 US-119, Putney, KY 40865, (606) 573-9009 Harlan County Shriners on Facebook.

Getting There

To Shuttle Point/Take-out: The take-out and put-in are located 10 miles apart along U.S. 119 in Harlan County.

The take-out is at the Shriner's Park, near the playground. The Park is on Shriner's Road on the south side of the river, also on the south side of U.S. 119 at Putney. The park is open to the public from dawn until dusk.

The Shriner's Park is accessed off county road 1002c. From the park, follow Co. Road 1002c for 0.2 mile to Ky. 522, and then turn right. After 0.6 miles, when you reach the intersection of Ky. 2010, turn right. In 0.2 mile, when you reach U.S. 119, turn left to travel north for 8.6 miles to Morris Bottom Road on the right.

The put-in is next to the bridge on upriver side, on the southern bank. Parking is located between the river and U.S. 119.

The Poor Fork of the Cumberland River passes through a wide river valley in southeast Kentucky, providing views of life in the southern coalfields. CARRIE STAMBAUGH

River Overview

The Poor Fork of the Cumberland River begins in western Virginia and flows through the Cumberland Mountains of southeast Kentucky on its way to its confluence with the Big South Fork of the Cumberland River and then on to Lake Cumberland. Its bed is comprised of rock and gravel, creating some small shoals and rapids that make the paddling fun. The water often flows crystal clear and lateral erosion is minimal on the river, so downfalls are atypical. Exposed rock and frequent panoramic views of the surrounding forested mountains make this paddle a true gem.

The Paddle

This paddle begins at the roadside of U.S. 119 just north of the town of Harlan. It lies at the foot of Pine Mountain, a ridge that stretches unbroken for more than 125 miles from Virginia through Kentucky to Tennessee.

The paddle begins just before the bridge at Morris Bottom Road and U.S. 119. The put-in is down a small, grassy bank with gravel, but it can become muddy in wet weather and after heavy rains.

Immediately after putting in, float under the first of many bridges along this paddle. At mile 0.4, in low water levels, there is a rocky shoal that extends the width of the river, but it is runnable. A farm with several horses is located on river right.

At mile 0.9, the river crosses under the first U.S. 119 bridge. At mile 1.1, the river passes under a wooden hanging footbridge that is clearly not in use anymore. Here the railroad joins the road in paralleling the river as you follow a curve in the river and come to the bridge. The railroad is on the north side, and U.S. 119 is on the south, or river left.

After some more bumpy shoals at mile 1.7, there is a big rock outcropping on the inside of the bend. There is a nice, deep pool here, most likely holding nice size rock bass. At mile 2.0, the river crosses beneath U.S. 119 once again, and at mile 2.3, a private road crosses the river too, before U.S. 119 crosses again at mile 2.5 as the road shifts back to river left. As you pass under the bridge here, some rocky shoals should be navigated to river left.

At mile 3.0, the river bends to the right and passes beneath the first of two coal tipples on this stretch. A coal tipple is a structure used to separate and load extracted coal onto railcar hopper cars for transport. A long, conveyor belt–type structure carries the coal across the river and into a large warehouse structure where it is separated and loaded for transport.

At mile 3.4, the river passes over an old road, which in high water creates a low head dam. At low water levels, it can be easily navigated to river left. At moderate water levels and above, it could create a significant navigational hazard, especially if debris is caught on it. Portage should be made to river left.

Active coal tipples on the banks of the Poor Fork provide a glimpse of the local industry from the water. CARRIE STAMBAUGH

At mile 3.5, the river passes beneath U.S. 119, as the road shifts to the south side of the river before it shifts again to the north at mile 4. (The railroad is on the south side of the river here, or river right.)

At mile 4.7 and 4.8, the river passes beneath a pair of conveyor belts carrying coal to and from a second coal tipple. Beware of a large pile of river debris on the south bank—the same side as the coal tipple.

At mile 6, U.S. 119 crosses over the river again just downstream from the remnants of a previous bridge. The railroad and road are now both on the south side of the river. At mile 6.3 is a second bridge. Just before reaching the second bridge is a small island. It should be navigated to river right, where a small wave train provides a bit of excitement and momentum.

Downriver from here a set of rocky shoals requires navigating in a zigzag from river right to river left and back before crossing again under U.S. 119 at mile 8.1. At mile 8.5, the river crosses under yet another bridge, and the river curves quickly back to the left.

At mile 9.6 is a small rapid with a small recirculating hydraulic that is possible to "surf" and is easily navigable to river right. At mile 9.8, the river crosses under U.S.

Poor Fork of the Cumberland River

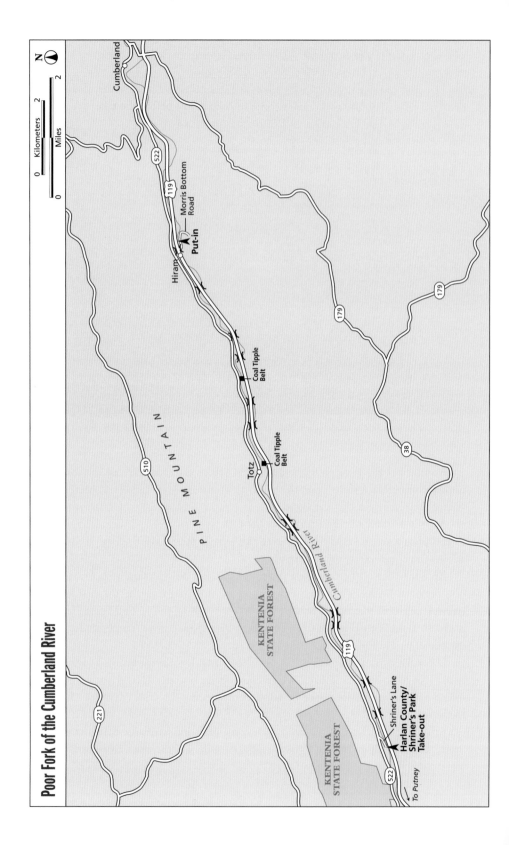

N

0   Kilometers   2

0   Miles   2

Cumberland

522

119

Morris Bottom
Road

Hiram

▲ **Put-in**

Coal Tipple
Belt

Coal Tipple
Belt

Totz

510

221

P I N E   M O U N T A I N

KENTENIA
STATE FOREST

KENTENIA
STATE FOREST

Cumberland River

119

179

179

38

Shriner's Lane

**Harlan County/
Shriner's Park
Take-out**

522

To Putney

119 again and then again at mile 10.5, where another wave trail on the river right can easily push an inattentive paddler into a bridge pylon.

The take-out is just over a half-mile further at mile 11.1 on river right. The Shriner's playground and a few benches come into view, just before the take-out. During early spring, the horse corral is visible too, but in the summer, it could be hidden by foliage. A power line also crosses the river at the take-out.

9 Ohio River Manchester Islands

This is an easy paddle that gives boaters a chance to experience the natural beauty and wildlife of the Ohio River and its few remaining islands. The paddle is a loop, with the put-in and take-out at the same location. It circumnavigates the larger of the two islands, passing through the navigation channel dividing the two, and makes a stop on a popular sandy beach on the small island.

County: Lewis
Start and End: Island Creek Marina and Campground, 8801 U.S. 52, Manchester, Ohio. N 38 41.448', W 83 34.959'
Note: The boat ramp for this paddle is located in Ohio. Kentucky owns the Ohio River from its shore to the historic low water mark on the northern-most bank, making this paddle almost entirely within the Commonwealth of Kentucky.
Length: 3.5 miles
Float Time: 2.5 hours
Difficulty: Moderate
Rapids: I
River Type: Level controlled, commercial waterway
Current: Moderate
River Gradient: None

River Gauge: http://www.lrh-wc.usace.army .mil/wm/?river/ohio—Maysville
Land Status: Public/private
Nearest Cities/Towns: Manchester, Ohio / Maysville, Kentucky
Boats Used: Canoe, Kayak, SUP
Season: Any
Fees or Permits: Island Creek is privately owned. It costs $4 to launch a canoe or kayak from the boat ramp here.
Maps: USGS Manchester Islands
Organizations: US Army Corps of Engineers, Huntington District
Contacts/Outfitters: Island Creek Marina and Campground, 8801 U.S. 52, Manchester, Ohio 45144, (937) 549-1430; www.islandcreek marina.webs.com; islandcreekmarina@gmail .com

Getting There

To Put-in/Take-out: Take U.S. 68 from Maysville, Kentucky, crossing the Ohio River to Ohio where U.S. 68 joins U.S. 52. Turn right to head east. Drive 11.7 miles, passing through the community of Manchester. The Island Creek Marina and Campground is on the right just before the highway crosses Island Creek.

River Overview

The mighty Ohio River defines the northern border of Kentucky from its confluence with the Big Sandy River at Catlettsburg, Kentucky, until it empties into the Mississippi River just north of Wickliffe, Kentucky. The Ohio River is 981 miles long. It begins in Pittsburgh, Pennsylvania, where the Monongahela and Allegheny Rivers meet, and it ends at Cairo, Illinois, where it is the single largest tributary of the

The channel between the Manchester Islands is wide but used for commerical traffic.
CARRIE STAMBAUGH

Mississippi River. The Ohio River drains fifteen states, an area of more than 189,000 square miles, and provides drinking water to more than three million Americans.

The Ohio River played a major role in Native American life and in the settlement and early economic development of the United States. It remains a vital transportation corridor to this day with barges hauling millions of tons of freight up and down the river annually.

Locks and dams began being built along the Ohio River as early as the 1830s, when a canal was built to bypass the Falls of the Ohio at Louisville, and by the 1950s, there were nineteen locks and dams on the river, which the US Army Corps of Engineers now manage. These man-made structures have broken the river into twenty-one pools of slow-moving and nearly constantly navigable waterways.

The Paddle

It takes only a couple of hours to circumnavigate both islands, which combined comprise just less than 120 acres. After launching from the boat ramp, I quickly paddled the approximately quarter mile across the river to the large island using a downriver ferry angle. I choose to paddle downriver alongside the large island before

The Ohio River Manchester Islands are National Wildlife Refuge Areas. The smallest island offers a sandy beach, popular with all kinds of recreational boaters. CARRIE STAMBAUGH

OHIO RIVER ISLANDS NATIONAL WILDLIFE REFUGE

The Manchester Islands are part of the Ohio River Islands National Wildlife Refuge, a network of twenty-five protected islands along the river, which are open to the public between sunrise and sunset daily. Many of the river's islands, created from natural gravel and sand deposits, have long disappeared, but several, including the two featured in this paddle, have survived and are now protected as vital habitat for a variety of native species. The Manchester Islands are the two southernmost protected islands on the Ohio River and the only two within Kentucky's jurisdiction; the remaining twenty-three are located upriver in West Virginia waters.

turning upriver to paddle in the channel between the two islands because the current between the southern bank and the islands is not as strong as it is on the northern side of the islands. By the time I crossed the river, I was at about the midpoint of the island, which is approximately 1.5 miles long.

The banks of the large island are approximately 10 feet high, steep, muddy, and heavily wooded. The overhanging trees from the large island provided some welcome shade during our late afternoon paddle. We noticed a handful of pawpaws floating near the bank, and upon further investigation, we startled a muskrat that quickly headed underwater to avoid us.

The southern end of the island has a shallow, gentle, sloping bank, which makes a good place to land to explore the island by foot. A navigational beacon is located at the end of the island.

Turning around the end of the island and heading up river, a picnic table quickly comes into view on river left. (The second Manchester Island is now visible upriver on river right, or the southern bank of the river.) The current was mild, and paddling against it did not require much effort.

A number of gravel beaches can be found on this side of the river, with trees extending out over the water. We saw a small fawn drinking from the river in the shade of one such tree and noted numerous blue herons wading in the shallow water off the island as well. Wildflowers, including butterfly milkweed, attract a number of native butterflies and songbirds, including the endangered Monarch butterfly.

As we approached the northern end of the first island and the southern end of the second island, at mile 1.8, we again used a ferry angle to cross to the second island.

The channel is 0.2 mile wide, and at mile 2.0, you can reach a natural sandy beach on the smaller island. It stretches about 100 yards. This is a popular spot for anchoring recreational crafts, and it is not uncommon for dozens of boaters to be anchored here. The generally calm waters in the eddy of the island are ideal for swimming, and the sand makes a great playground for little ones! A trail also heads into the interior of the island from the beach.

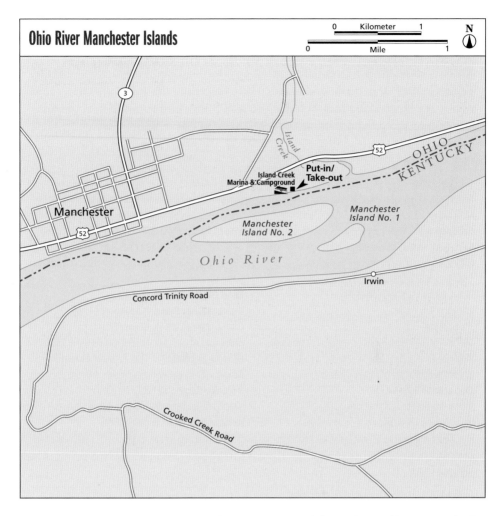

Ohio River Manchester Islands

A note of caution for paddling this area: Tows with large fleets of barges attached do frequently pass through the area. Pay attention to them, and remember to stay out of their way, and prepare for their wake when paddling a small pleasure craft. In the time I spent on the water during this Sunday paddle, only a single tow passed by, providing a welcome photo opportunity. Downriver traffic uses the northern channel, but upriver traffic passes between the two islands.

From the beach, it is a half-mile paddle to the northern end of the small island, which serves as a good point to begin crossing the Ohio River—about 0.7 mile wide here—to head back toward the northern bank. Then paddle downstream to the take-out. This makes for a round-trip of approximately 3.5 miles.

10 Kinniconick Creek

This is a pleasant 7.5-mile paddle on the upper section of the creek through pastoral Lewis County. Deep pools hold trophy muskellunge, and the water often flows clear over a gravel, mud, and rock bottom. The only bridge on the paddle is at the take-out, making it a remote and quiet paddle. The most common obstacles are frequent logjams, some of which create some potentially dangerous strainers.

County: Lewis
Start: Leatherwood Park, Ky. 59, 6241 Fairlane Drive, Vanceburg, KY
N 38 30.628', W 83 19.640'
End: Behind Globe Funeral Chapel of Lewis, at intersection of Lower Kinney Road (Co. Road 1104) and Ky. 59
N 38 29.048', W 83 16.889'
Length: 7.5 miles
Float Time: 3 hours
Difficulty: Moderate due to potential portages
Rapids: I
River Type: Rocky, pastoral stream
Current: Slow to swift
River Gradient: 2.3 feet per mile

River Gauge: There is no gauge on the creek. It is recommended paddlers check the gauge on the Tygarts Creek and do a visual check of the river before paddling. When the gauge on the Tygarts Creek is flowing between 50 and 130 cfs (2.5 to 3.5 feet), the Kinniconick is good to paddle.
Land Status: Private
Nearest City/Town: Vanceburg
Boats Used: Canoe, Kayak, SUP
Season: Late winter, spring, after heavy rains
Fees or Permits: No fees or permits required
Maps: USGS Vanceburg, Head of Grassy
Organizations: Kentucky Department of Fish and Wildlife: https://fw.ky.gov/Fish/Pages/Kinniconick_Creek.aspx#ACC01

Getting There

To Shuttle point/Take-out: From Greenup, travel 5 miles on U.S. 23 North to the intersection of the AA Highway (Ky. 10), and then turn left to go west. After 24 miles, Ky. 10 merges with Ky. 9 and becomes Ky. 9 North. After three miles, turn left onto Ky. 59 South. After five miles, pass the junction of County Road 344, taking a slight left to continue on Ky. 59. In 5 miles, turn left onto Lower Kinni Road (County Road 1102) and park in a large gravel lot at Globe Funeral Chapel, 7975 Lower Kinni Road, Vanceburg, Kentucky.

To Put-in from Take-out: Retrace your steps back on Ky. 59 North for 3.7 miles, then turn left to enter Leatherwood Park. The park has a picnic shelter with a green aluminum roof, picnic tables, and room for a dozen cars.

Follow the telephone wire 0.1 mile back to the creek, and turn left to access the river.

The Kinniconick is one of Kentucky's greatest natural muskellunge (muskie) fishing streams.
CARRIE STAMBAUGH

River Overview

Kinniconick Creek flows 99 miles across Lewis County before entering the Ohio River at Garrison. "The Kinni," as locals call it, has long been regarded as one of the state's best muskellunge fishing creeks with its deep pools between shallow riffles and abundant rock bars. Abundant populations of smallmouth bass, spotted bass, rock bass, and other fish make it an excellent location for the paddler who wants to do some fishing too. Local lore says the best time to paddle and fish the creek is in the early spring "when the bluebells bloom."

The Kinniconick passes through pastoral Lewis County, offering a quiet summer paddle.
Carrie Stambaugh

Kinniconick Creek

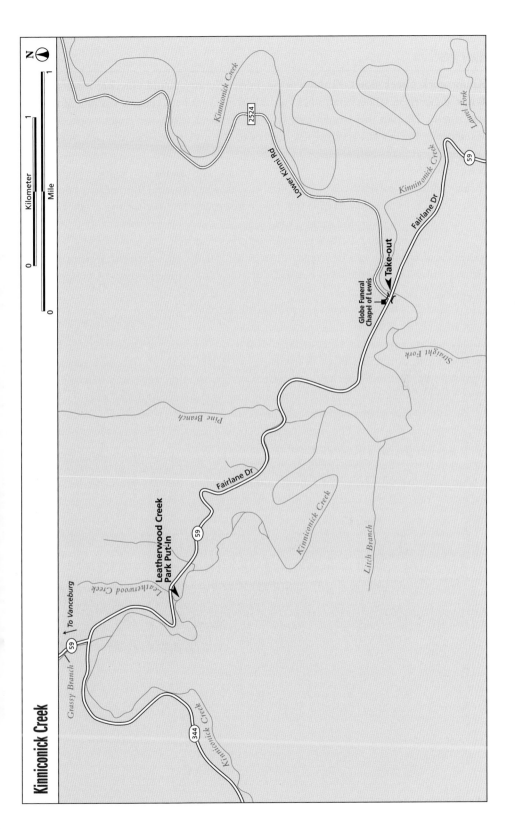

The Paddle

Kinniconick snakes its way through delightfully quiet countryside. Its deep pools are shaded by large hemlocks and other hardwoods separated by series of shallow shoals and ripples. Despite the presence of homes and farms along the creek, noticeably absent along the creek is trash—quite impressive for a waterway that regularly floods! Paddlers should use caution as the waterway did flood in early 2017, creating a number of new logjams.

From the put-in, the river is about 40 feet wide and separated from nearby homes with a steep, muddy bank. At mile 0.9, a large tree spans the river, forcing paddlers to portage to river right on the rocky bank.

Large trees including hemlocks shade the creek—at mile 1.6, a particularly large specimen of hemlock can be found on river left, on the embankment. River right features a pleasant farm field. Just beyond it, at mile 1.8, is another logjam that requires portaging to the right.

At mile 2.8, the river crosses a shallow water crossing. Beware of nearby farm dogs who like to greet paddlers and follow them down the river! The banks here are muddy and approximately 5 feet high on river left while it slopes up to the ridge top on river right. A number of small tributaries enter the creek on this stretch, falling over rocks to meet the waterway. Kingfishers were a common sight on this stretch, as were a number of other waterfowl, including herons and mallard ducks.

At mile 4.9, just after a narrow rocky shoal, is a dangerous logjam. The river should be portaged on the right. The river then widens and deepens before narrowing once again and making another curve at mile 6. There are excellent fishing coves along this section of river, where grassy fields slope down to the water's edge. Private camps dot it with small fishing docks on river left, and river right is heavily wooded, but there are plenty of small flats and rocky banks to stop for a riverside lunch or to stretch one's legs.

At mile 7.3, in a particularly scenic area of woods, the river makes yet another S curve and narrows, and the highway bridge comes into sight. Cross under the bridge and take-out on river left on the grassy bank below the Globe Funeral Home.

11 Tailwaters of Cave Run Lake (Middle Fork of the Licking River)

This is an easy paddle on a slow-moving, deep stretch of the Middle Fork of the Licking River. The paddle begins at the spillway of Cave Run Lake and ends just past the U.S. 60 Bridge outside of the small town of Farmers. There are numerous campgrounds along the paddle, which also passes the Minor E. Clark State Fish Hatchery.

Counties: Rowan, Bath
Start: Cave Run Lake Spillway and Dam
N 38 07.058', W 83 32.326'
End: U.S. 60 Bridge
N 38 08.397', W 83 33.481'
Length: 4 miles
Float Time: 1.5 hours
Difficulty: Easy
Rapids: I
River Type: Rural, farm-bordered river with steep, muddy embankments
Current: Moderate
River Gradient: 1.2 feet per mile
River Gauge: USGS 03249505 Licking River at U.S. 60, Farmers, Ky.
   Visit http://lrl-apps.lrl.usace.army.mil/wc/reports/lkreport.html to check flow levels from the Cave Run Dam. The minimum release from the dam should be 120 cfs.

Land Status: Public/private
Nearest City/Town: Farmers
Boats Used: Canoe, Kayak, SUP
Season: Summer through early spring
Fees or Permits: $3 day pass for parking in Daniel Boone National Forest
Maps: USGS Salt Lick, Farmers
Organizations/Contacts: US Army Corps of Engineers, 150 Ky. 826, Morehead, KY 40351, (606) 784-9709
   U.S. Forest Service, Cumberland Ranger District, Daniel Boone National Forest, 2375 Ky. 801 South, Morehead, KY 40351, (606) 784-6428
Outfitters: The Ole Cornfield, 922 Cave Run Road, Salt Lick, KY 40373, theOleCornfield.com; (606) 356-5605

Getting There

To Shuttle Point/Take-out: I-64 to exit 133, Ky. 801. Follow Ky. 801 South for three miles, and then turn right onto U.S. 60 West. After a half mile, you cross over the Licking River. The take-out is on the right just below the bridge. An access road here ends on private property, so be mindful to park along the shoulder of the road.
To Put-in from Takeout: Retrace your steps a half mile back to the intersection of U.S. 60 and Ky. 801 South. Turn right to follow the road toward the tailwaters area, and then after 2 miles, turn right onto Ky. 826. After crossing over the dam, in 1 mile, take the first road on the right. Follow the signs to the boat ramp.

The Middle Fork of the Licking River leaves Cave Run Lake as a wide, sluggish river.
CARRIE STAMBAUGH

River Overview

The Licking River flows more than 320 miles from southeast Kentucky to its confluence with the Ohio River in Newport, Kentucky, across from Cincinnati, Ohio. The river was called the Great Salt Creek by early pioneers because of the numerous natural salt licks found along its banks. The river was used as a natural transportation passageway for Native Americans and early settlers. Today, the river is essentially split in two by Cave Run Lake in southern Bath County. Below the dam, where this paddle is, the river passes through rolling pasturelands and small forests. More than a hundred species of fish and fifty species of mussels can be found in the waterway.

The Paddle

This is a great little paddle on the river and is easy to combine with a trip on the lake for a multiday paddle and camping trip. There are no large powerboats on this stretch of the river, making it quieter and friendlier for families.

The paddle starts at the boat ramp immediately below the lake's dam. Here the Middle Fork of the Licking River is approximately 50 feet wide and deeply shaded by large hardwood trees. The waters are calm as they begin to snake their way away

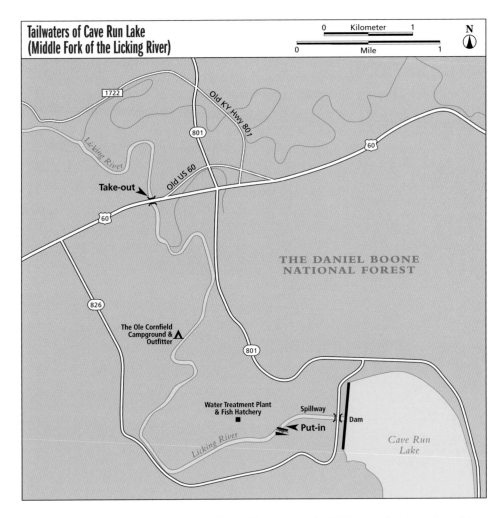

from the river toward Kentucky's rolling Bluegrass region. This stretch is popular with human and avian anglers, including the blue heron. The banks are 10 feet high and grassy along this stretch, sloping gently down to the river.

Power lines cross the river at mile 0.2, and the water level gauge is at mile 0.3 on river left. At mile 0.7, private homes come into view above the river, many with large sets of wooden stairs leading up the hills to decks. A few logjams dot the river but are easy to navigate, as is a large grassy island at mile 1.4.

At mile 2.2, the river comes around a curve and immediately passes on river left a series of docks laden with canoes and kayaks, with stairs leading up to campsites above the river. This is the Ole Cornfield Campground and Outfitter. The river continues to wind past private homes, and at mile 2.8, it passes the water treatment plant before passing beneath a second set of power lines.

The current is sluggish here, and the edges of the river are mostly shaded, but large turtles can be seen sunning themselves on logs where the sunlight filters through the trees along the banks and on logjams in the center of the waterway.

At mile 3.1, the river makes a curve around a rock bar with a large sycamore tree at its center. The roadway is visible in this stretch, but soon, the river moves away from the road and becomes quieter for a stretch.

At mile 3.9, the U.S. 60 Bridge comes into view. The take-out is under the bridge on river left across from the discharge pipe on river right and before concrete pylons of a former bridge.

12 Red River

The Red River Gorge section of the Red River is an easy, spectacularly scenic paddle through the heart of one of Kentucky's most well-known and popular hiking and climbing areas. This paddle cannot be beat for the views of soaring rock formations, riverside boulders, gravel bars, and mature forest, as well as ease of access and shuttle.

At low levels, this paddle can easily become a hike, and even at flows of 200, sections of the river are very shallow and require maneuverability. I misjudged the depth of the river at several points and found myself sitting on a gravel bar. Only once, however, did I have to abandon ship and drag my boat back into deeper water.

The float begins beneath the bridge on Sky Bridge Road in the heart of the Red River Gorge recreation area and continues for 8 miles to the old "Silver Bridge" where Ky. 77 (Tar Ridge Road) crosses the Red River at its intersection with Ky. 613 and near the terminus of Ky. 715.

Counties: Wolfe, Menifee, Powell
Start: Copperas Creek Boat Launch
N 37 49.175', W 83 34.504'
End: Ky. 77/ Ky. 715 a.k.a. "The Silver Bridge"
N 37 49.993', W 83 39.608'
Length: 8 miles
Float Time: 3.5 hours
Difficulty: Moderate
Rapids: I+
River Type: Narrow, rocky mountain stream
Current: Moderate to fast
River Gradient: 2.5 feet per mile
River Gauge: USGS Gauge: 03283500 Red River at Clay City Minimum: 180 cfs—max. flood (cfs), the best flow is around 250 cfs

Land Status: Public
Nearest City: Slade
Boat Used: Kayak, Canoe
Season: Fall to early summer, after heavy rain
Fees or Permits: None
Maps: Slade, Pomeroyton
Organizations: Daniel Boone National Forest Gladie Visitor Center, 3451 Sky Bridge Road, Stanton, KY 40380, (606) 663-8100
Contacts/Outfitter: Red River Adventures Canoe and Kayak Rental & Campground, www.KyPaddle.com, (606) 663-1012

Getting There

To Shuttle Point/Take-out: From Slade or the Bert T. Combs Mountain Parkway, take Ky. 11 North for 1.5 miles, crossing the Red River. A small pull-out and path to the take-out are located immediately after the right turn onto Ky. 77 North from the bridge. There is room for one or two cars. There is a parking lot to the left of the bridge on North Fork Road.

To Put-in from Take-out: The Copperas Creek Canoe Carry-down with parking is located 7.6 miles from the take-out on Ky. 715. From the take-out, follow Ky. 77 for 0.8 miles. Then continue straight on Ky. 715 for 6.9 miles. Parking for the launch

The "middle section" of the Red River winds through one of the most scenic stretches of the Red River Gorge Geological Area. CARRIE STAMBAUGH

is on the left immediately before the bridge. The carry-down is across the road and down a small set of stairs, also before the bridge.

River Overview

The Red River is Kentucky's only federally designated Wild and Scenic River. A 19.7-mile stretch of the river, including the entire paddle detailed here, is within the federally-designated area. A 9-mile stretch of the river is designated a Kentucky Wild River, beginning from the same point the federal designation does but ending just upstream from the put-in for this paddle.

Originating in Wolfe County, the Red River flows northwest briefly, forming the border of Menifee and Powell Counties, before flowing through Powell County and then for a short time creates the boundary between Estill and Clark Counties before it meets the Kentucky River south of Winchester in Estill County.

For paddling purposes, the river is divided into three sections: the upper, middle, and lower. The upper section is a gorgeous Class II–III whitewater run but is not for novices. The narrow stream flows through steep stone bluffs and is known to become

THE RED RIVER GORGE

The Red River Gorge Geological Area is an exceptionally scenic area of the Daniel Boone National Forest, noted for its abundance of natural arches, rock shelters, sandstone cliffs, and other unusual rock formations. There are more than a hundred natural arches in the area, sculpted by both wind and water. It is designated a National Geological Area by the US Forest Service.

The area is also archeologically significant. The first people to inhabit the area arrived 13,000 years ago during the last ice age and around 3,000 years ago began to cultivate early domesticated crops in plots here. In 2003, the Red River Gorge, adjoining Clifty Wilderness Area and the Indian Creek area of the Daniel Boone National Forest, was declared a National Archeological District and placed on the National Register of Historic Places.

White settlers also called the area home, and the Gladie Cabin is a reconstruction of a 1800s log house. The land on which it sits, next to Gladie Creek, was used for subsistence farming and later as a logging camp for the surrounding timber industry.

The nearby Nada Tunnel, nicknamed Gateway to the Gorge, was constructed in 1910 for a narrow-gauge railway to carry timber 15 miles to the sawmill at Clay City. Today, it is a one-way section of Ky. 77, which carries two-way traffic through the gorge. It is 12 feet wide, 13 feet high, and 900 feet long, so large RVs and large tour buses cannot access it. It is listed on the National Historic Registry.

Hiking and rock climbing are both popular activities in the gorge. Park rangers stress to visitors to be careful around and mindful of the cliff ledges that make the area so scenic. The cliffs average 100 feet in height, and a fall can be fatal. On average one visitor is killed or seriously injured every year in a fall. Visitors shouldn't get too close or camp near edges. Walking or hiking in the dark is strongly discouraged and visitors should not engage in "risky" behavior. Alcoholic beverages are prohibited.

obstructed by deadfalls; its rapids are not terribly technical, but they leave little room for error.

The middle section of the river flows through the center of the Red River Gorge Geological Area, passing Sky Bridge Arch, Tower Rock, and Chimney Top Rock. The paddling is much friendlier to family paddling, but sharp turns, large boulders, small ledges, and sand and rock shoals make for an interesting paddle.

The lower section of the Red River flows for a few miles through the Daniel Boone National Forest before it leaves public lands and flows between hilly farmland

and private woodlands on its way to meet the Kentucky River. The river can become chocked with deadfalls, and there are many bridges crossing the river.

The Paddle

The launch is just above the mouth of Copperas Creek. A nice drop-off loop exists at the bottom, and there is a decent parking area. The launch has a set of stone steps, which are a bit treacherous on their own because they lean at the bottom where the bank has begun to erode.

The paddle begins on the river beneath the sky bridge itself and makes a wide horseshoe bend around Hen's Nest Rock, which comes into view immediately but disappears over the next 0.6 mile. Just before the river begins to curve north at the end of that ridge again, at mile 1.8, both sides of the river are littered with logs displaying the natural power of the river when the water rises. Stay in the middle of the stream to avoid any collisions here with unseen snags.

Large boulders and lush hardwood forest dominate the landscape of the Red River as it flows through the Red River Gorge Geological Area. CARRIE STAMBAUGH

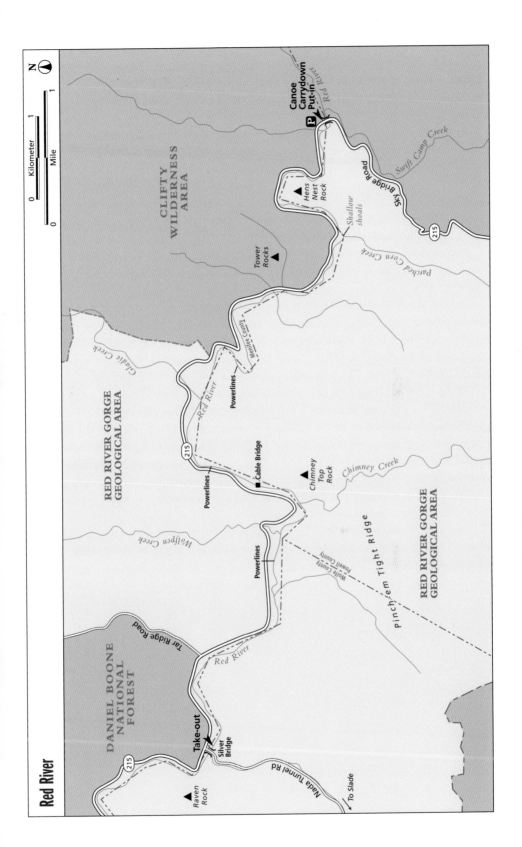

At the 2-mile mark, Parched Corn Creek comes in from the south on river left. A shallow shoal of rocks marks the confluence; stay well to river right here to catch the current and slide past. As the river completes its turn, be sure to look up to catch another glimpse of high exposed rocks down river.

As this lazy horseshoe finishes and the river prepares for a much tighter turn at mile 3, a pair of tributaries comes in from both sides: Sal Branch on river right, and Laurel Branch on river left. Above the river on river right, the ridge rises to 1,166 feet.

A tight horseshoe turn in the river follows as you curve around the ridge, and then the river straightens out for its longest straight stretch of the paddle. Gladie Creek glides into the Red at mile 4. Notice the tiny wooden structure on river right.

Remember to look up from time to time to see Sky Splitter as you paddle straight at it before it disappears into the trees as you glide beneath it, and the river begins a southerly straight stretch.

To river left is the Princess Arch area of the forest, and soon, the cable bridge that the Sheltowee Trace National Recreation Trail uses to cross the Red River comes into view at mile 5. High above, on river left, soar the Chimney Top Rocks. Chimney Top Creek comes in on river left. Again, be sure to look up to search for the top of Pinch-Em Tight Ridge, which briefly comes into view high above the river.

At mile 7, just before Dunkirk Branch comes in from river right, is Red River Adventures campground and take-out. Straight ahead is Ravens Rock.

The public take-out under the bridge is another mile down the river on the right just before the creek passes under the Ky. 77 Bridge. This bridge marks the intersection of Ky. 77 and Ky. 613 (also known as Forestry Road No. 23, which parallels the road for the next 9 miles on river right).

The path out is narrow and quickly turns into a stream during rains. It is also lined with stinging nettle and poison ivy.

There is a small pull-out on the road next to the river at the entrance to the bridge. There is a path leading down to the riverbank, but it is steep and muddy. Use caution in this corner. There is a trailhead parking area across the road on forest service land. Use the pull-out for loading and unloading only.

13 Middle Fork of the Licking River

This is a paddle on a quiet, protected stretch of the Licking River between two of its most famous licks: the Upper and Lower Blue Licks. The paddling is easy—only a few bumpy shoals to navigate. The banks are muddy and tree-lined, and the water is teaming with fish. This stretch of river is historically significant because it is just above where the last battle of the American Revolution is supposed to have taken place. The site of the battlefield, just downstream from this paddle's take-out, is preserved as Blue Licks State Park.

Counties: Nicholas, Fleming
Start: Upper Blue Licks Boat Ramp
N 38 19.981', W 83 51.429'
End: Clay Wildlife Management Area Canoe Carrydown
N 38 21.935', W 83 55.986'
Length: 10 miles
Float Time: 3.5 hours
Difficulty: Moderate
Rapids: I
River Type: Rural, farm-bordered river with steep muddy embankments
Current: Moderate
River Gradient: 1.1 feet per mile
River Gauge: USGS Blue Licks Springs. The reading needs to be at 150 cfs or higher.

Land Status: Public
Nearest City/Town: Carlisle
Boats Used: Canoe, Kayak, SUP
Season: Any
Fees or Permits: None
Maps: USGS Moorefield, Sherburne
Organizations/Contacts/Outfitters: Blue Licks Battlefield State Resort Park, 10299 Maysville Road, Carlisle, KY 40311, (859) 289-5507
Kentucky Department of Fish and Wildlife Resources, Clay Wildlife Management Area, 1449 Cassidy Creek Road, Carlisle, KY 40311, (859) 289-8564 www.fw.ky.gov/education/pages/Licking-River.aspx

---

Getting There

To Shuttle Point/Take-out: From Carlisle, take Ky. 32 6.5 miles to Mexico Road, and then turn right. Clay Wildlife Management Area Canoe Carrydown is located 1 mile above the intersection of Mexico Road and State Route 32 on the right.

To Put-In from Take-out: Turn left onto Mexico Road, travel 1 mile, and then turn left onto Ky. 32. Cross the Licking River, then cross a second Bridge and turn left onto Ky. 57 and enter the Clay WMA after a half mile. Travel south on Ky. 57, and at mile 3.3, you pass a WMA boat ramp on the left. Continue on Ky. 57 until mile 6.7, which is the junction of Ky. 3315 (Cassidy Creek Road). Turn left, and then go up a steep hill. At mile 9.6, reach the put-in on the left; it is a short drive down a gravel road.

River Overview

The Licking River flows more than 320 miles from southeast Kentucky to its confluence with the Ohio River in Newport, Kentucky, across from Cincinnati, Ohio. The river was called the Great Salt Creek by early pioneers because of the numerous natural salt licks found along its banks. Prehistoric animals including woolly mammoths and giant mastodons visited these licks along with animals we would recognize today, including bison, elk, and deer.

The river was used as a natural transportation passageway for Native Americans and early settlers and today is one of Kentucky's most beloved recreational rivers in part for its native muskellunge fishery. Smallmouth and spotted bass are also abundant on this stretch of river.

The Paddle

The paddle begins at the Upper Blue Licks and winds its way through the Clay Wildlife Management Area to a canoe carrydown just as the river exits the WMA. The river is wide, approximately 60 to 70 feet on this stretch, relatively calm, and shaded by large trees for most of this paddle, making it perfect for a mid-summer day trip.

THE BATTLE OF BLUE LICKS

The Battle of Blue Licks was fought on August 19, 1782, and occurring 10 months after the surrender of General Charles Cornwallis at Bunker Hill, it was one of the last battles of the Revolutionary War.

Earlier in the month, a force of fifty British and Canadian Loyalists along with Native Americans made a raid from southern Ohio into Kentucky near Bryant's Station. The fort was well defended, so the force withdrew. But a force of 182 Kentucky militiamen, including pioneer Daniel Boone, set out in pursuit.

Upon reaching a spring and salt lick known as Lower Blue Licks at a crossing on the Licking River, the militiamen observed some natives run over a hill. Despite Boone advising the soldiers to make a flanking maneuver to avoid being ambushed in the nearby ravines, they continued pursuing the enemy. As soon as the settlers came within easy gun range, the British, Canadians, and around 300 Native Americans opened fire.

During the disorganized retreat that followed, seventy Kentuckians, including Boone's son Israel, along with militia leader Stephen Trigg and leader Colonel John Todd, were killed. Many of the settlers were hacked down by tomahawks, and their bodies were later mutilated. A force under Benjamin Logan met up with fleeing settlers and returned to the battlefield several days later to bury the dead.

The Middle Fork of the Licking River played an important role in early American pioneer history and makes for an excellent summer paddling destination. CARRIE STAMBAUGH

The Middle Fork of the Licking is a historic waterway, noted for its natural salt licks that draw wildlife. CARRIE STAMBAUGH

There are plenty of rocky shoals and low, muddy banks for picnicking and many fine, deep swimming holes along this paddle.

In fact, the put-in is located on a rocky shoal that served as an old fording place. The water can be quite shallow here, so navigate to the far right of the river to catch the current in deeper moving water as soon as possible. This is also a popular spot for horseback riders to water their horses, so be aware of your surroundings!

Several small rock and grass islands, including a particularly large one at mile 1, make the paddling interesting. Several small tributaries enter the river over the next mile, and at mile 2.2, the river enters a small straight stretch before continuing to wind its way downstream. Intermittent meadows break up the wooded stretches of the river. At mile 4.1, the river narrows to go around a rock island, which is marked by a large strainer on river left. Stay to the right.

At mile 5 is another rock island on river left as it bends; stay to the right again just before crossing under a set of power lines. As mentioned, this is an excellent fishing stream, and my husband spotted a good size muskie (more than 30 inches long) from his kayak on a day when the water was slightly muddy. We saw numerous bass jumping at insects throughout our afternoon and were treated to a few other creature sightings, including an array of birds and a swimming snake.

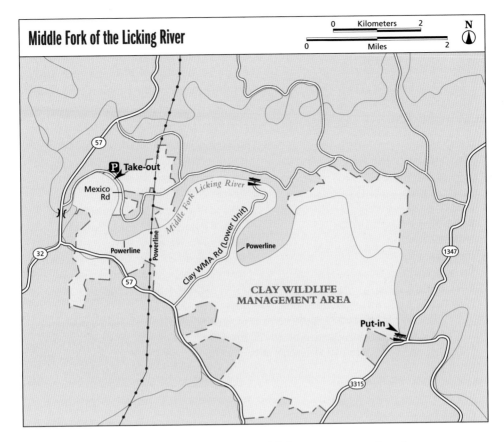

Middle Fork of the Licking River

At mile 6.7, you pass a second Clay Wildlife Management Area boat ramp on river left. At mile 8.7, the river passes under a set of high-tension power lines, the first of two within a half-mile stretch. The other set is at mile 9.1.

The river continues to alternate between straight stretches and bends, but ridges now rise approximately 60 feet on alternating sides of the river, creating a deep gorge-like feel, which is part of the reason Native Americans were able to surround and ambush the frontiersman during the Battle of Blue Licks.

At mile 10, reach the take-out on river right on a rock and grass bank. The parking lot at the take-out is 150 feet above the bank and is not visible from the river, so attention must be paid to locate the take-out.

14 Carr Creek Lake

This is an out-and-back loop paddle on the easternmost region of Carr Creek Lake. This paddle, mostly off the main lake, explores the Little Carr Fork region of the lake, including the region's signature marshlands.

County: Knott
Start and End: LittCarr Recreation Area Ramp N 37 14.146', W 82 57.152'
Length: 3 miles
Float Time: 2 hours
Rapids: None
Difficulty: Easy
River Type: Lake
Current: Slow
River Gradient: None
River Gauge: http://www.lrl-wc.usace.army .mil/reports/lkreport.html
   The lake maintains a summer pool of 1,028 feet, and it is lowered to a winter pool of 1,017 feet.

Land Status: Public
Nearest Cities/Towns: Hazard, Whitesburg
Boats Used: Canoe, Kayak, SUP
Season: Spring, summer, fall
Fees or Permits: $5 launch fee at LittCarr (waived if staying at the campground)
Maps: USGS Blackey
Organizations: US Army Corps of Engineers Louisville Carr Creek Lake Information Line: (606) 269-8164; Corps of Engineers office (606) 642-3308
   Carr Creek State Park, 2086 Smithboro Road, HWY 15, Sassafras, KY 41759, (606) 642-4050

Getting There

To Put-in/Take-out: From Hazard, take Ky. 15 south for 16 miles. Turn left onto Ky. 160 North. In 2 miles, just before the bridge over Carr Creek, turn left on to Boat Ramp Road to access ramp. This is the put-in/take-out. An alternative is the Carr Creek Campground, over the bridge, at the T intersection in 0.25 mile. Turn right. Cross creek again. There is carrydown access from many sites.

River Overview

Carr Creek Lake is a 710-acre impoundment of this tributary of the North Fork of the Kentucky River. The dam is located 8.8 miles north of the mouth of Carr Fork. Created by the US Army Corps of Engineers in 1976, it is a part of the massive Ohio River Basin Flood Control Plan. The lake provides drinking water for the surrounding communities.

   The marsh environment surrounding Carr Fork, rare in the eastern Kentucky mountains, provides habitat for a wide range of bird species including wood ducks, great blue herons, green herons, and kingfishers. The lake offers excellent fishing for crappie, catfish, bluegill, redbreast sunfish, and walleye.

Carr Creek Lake is nestled between steep wooded hills and includes a rare mountain marsh habitat. CARRIE STAMBAUGH

The area was home to some of the region's earliest settlers, and Carr Fork itself is believed to be named for William Carr, a well-known 1700s "Long Hunter." Carr was killed by Native Americans in the mid-1760s and was buried near the confluence of Breeding Creek and Carr Fork. His grave lies below the water of the lake that bears his name.

The lake is operated by the USACE, but much of the shoreline is protected as Carr Creek Wildlife Management Area and Carr Creek Lake State Park, which is located near the center of the lake.

The Paddle

This paddle begins and ends at the LittCarr boat ramp just off Ky. 160 and is inside the LittCarr Recreation Area. Many of the campsites in the LittCarr Campground have lake access. (I actually launched from site 19 on this particular paddle, which is the closest site to the boat ramp. It is a 0.28-mile paddle from the boat ramp to site 19.)

From the boat ramp, turn right to head northeast toward the campground, hugging the eastern bank. Along the way, one passes under the Ky. 160 Bridge, just

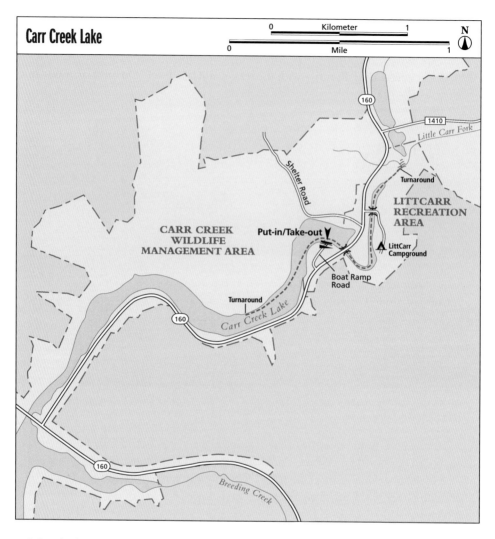

0.8 mile from the ramp. The western bank is lined with cattails and is gently sloping. There are picnic tables and boardwalks in this day use area. Note the number of nesting boxes along the shoreline. The eastern bank slopes steeply toward the ridge top and is heavily forested with a mix of hardwoods.

As it heads toward the campground, the steep bank gives way to a narrow plain and thick cattails appear on the eastern shore as well, hiding most of the campsites along the shore, although narrow coves allow access. The lake is narrow in this area—maybe 40 feet wide—and will continue to grow narrower as one heads toward the confluence of Little Carr Fork and Deadman Branch.

At mile 0.4, pass beneath the campground bridge. The steep, heavily wooded slope of the eastern bank returns. The western bank is low, with grasses and thick vegetation. As you make your way up the narrow waterway, the sound of rushing water will become louder and louder; stay to the right (eastern bank) as you pass the confluence of Deadman Branch, which enters from the northwest. At mile 0.65, you will reach the waterfall that marks the confluence of Little Carr with Carr Fork.

The height of the falls varies with the season and lake levels. On my visit, it was an approximately 8-foot-tall, stepped-stone waterfall that was flowing in at a high rate, creating a bit of a swirling current. At lower flows, this would be an excellent place to disembark and do a little exploring.

Turn around to head back to the main lake. (Deadman Branch can be explored only for a few hundred yards but was very active with fish on our visit, so it may be worth the time.) Heading back the way you came, you will reach the boat ramp at 1.3 miles. Continue past it into the now wider main body of the lake, which heads in a southwesterly direction. Ky. 160 hugs the southern shoreline high above the lake, and at times, it can create quite a bit of noise. The northern shore is heavily wooded with a steep bank. Walleye fishing is excellent here, however, as the lake is quite deep. Depending on the length of time one wants to spend on the water and on where one chooses to turn around, trips of varying lengths are possible.

I turned around at mile 2 (about 0.7 mile past the ramp) due to an impending thunderstorm to make an approximately 3-mile paddle.

15 Wood Creek Lake

This 625-acre lake partially within the Daniel Boone National Forest is a well-kept Kentucky secret for paddling and fishing. Explore the shallow coves for a chance to catch a trophy bass or just enjoy the scenery.

County: Laurel
Start and End: Wood Creek Ramp
N 37 11.142', W 84 10.614'
Length: 3.6 miles
Float Time: 3 hours
Difficulty: Easy
Rapids: None
River Type: Lake
Current: None
River Gradient: None
River Gauge: N/A
Land Status: Public/Private

Nearest City/Town: London
Boats Used: Canoe, Kayak, SUP
Season: Any
Fees or Permits: $3 parking fee at ramp
Maps: USGS Bernstadt
Organizations: Kentucky Department of Fish and Wildlife, (606) 878-5420
Contacts/Outfitters: Wood Creek Lake, 1 Wood Creek Lake Road, London, KY 40741, (606) 677-1098, info.center@ky.gov
    Wood Creek Lake Boat Dock, 1695 Moriah Road, London, KY 40741, (606) 878-5420

Getting There

To Put-in/Take-out: From I-75, take exit 41 to West Ky. 80. Follow for 7 miles to Hawk Creek Road, and then turn right. Then turn right Moriah Road, then right again at the intersection with Full Moon Circle Road. Moriah Road ends at the dock.

River Overview

Wood Creek Lake was created in 1969 by the damming of Wood Creek Lake. The lake lies partially within the DBNF and partially outside. It is the major source of drinking water for the nearby community. There are private docks and homes on the lake, and motorized crafts are allowed, but large houseboats and jet skis are not. Swimming is also prohibited. The fishing is superb. A state-record largemouth bass was pulled from this lake in 1984. It continues to offer excellent fishing for large and smallmouth bass, black and white crappie, sunfish, rainbow trout, and walleye.

The Paddle

This out-and-back loop paddle provided plenty of excitement in the form of active fishing in the middle of a summer day but was also serene and quiet in the heart of the busy lake tourism season.

Beginning at the boat ramp, head right or south along the western bank, passing the first cove that is lined with boat docks. With the exception of this area of the lake,

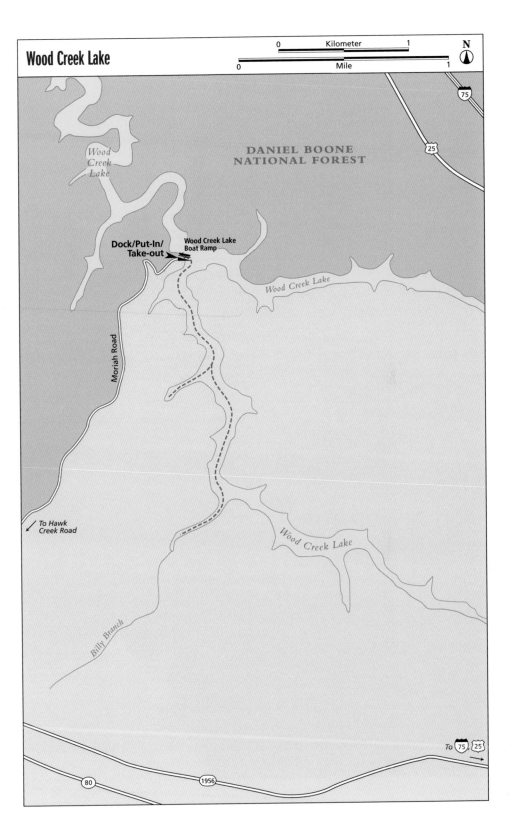

Wood Creek Lake's protected coves with standing trees are excellent places to fish for largemouth bass. CARRIE STAMBAUGH

which is heavy with docks, the rest of the lake boasts long stretches of shoreline without human development and with heavy vegetation. Other stretches of water feature private docks and boathouses, but overall, the lake retains a sleepy feel.

On our visit in the middle of July, we passed only two other motorized boats—small fishing "john boats" and a couple on SUP boards enjoying a cloudy paddle. When a sudden short rain shower blew up, it served to energize the lake's population of smallmouth bass.

This paddle explores several shallow coves along the western shoreline of the lake. The largest is 1.5 miles up the lake, at the back of which an area of standing trees and flooded button bushes are located. While fishing the standing timber, I lured in seven feisty largemouth bass—the largest topping out at over 4 pounds—in the span of 20 minutes all on a white spinner bait. It made for some of the most thrilling fishing of my life.

There is no telling how long that streak would have lasted if a thunderstorm with crackling lighting hadn't begun to blow up, forcing a speedy exit from the water. The paddle straight back to the ramp took about 30 minutes at a quick speed. Had the weather stayed calm and the fish active, it may have taken the remainder of the day.

16 Laurel River Lake

This paddle makes a loop on the easternmost section of the lake near the headwaters of the Laurel River. The put-in is near the Three Sisters Rock, which is popular for cliff-jumping. The paddle follows the main channel of the lake for a portion before circling back to the quiet headwater cove of the lake. This is an excellent paddle for fishing and swimming.

County: Laurel

Start and End: Laurel Bridge Recreation Area Ramp
N 36 58.142', W 84 07.639'

Distance: 5.5 miles

Float Time: 3 hours

Difficulty: Easy

Rapids: None

River Type: Lake

Current: Little near the dam

River Gradient: None

River Gauge: No

Land Status: Public

Nearest City/Town: Corbin

Boats Used: Canoe, Kayak, SUP

Season: Spring, summer, fall

Fees or Permits: Daniel Boone National Forest Day Pass required for parking at Laurel River Bridge Recreation Area. Fees are $3 per day, $5 for three days, and/or $30 annual pass.

Maps: USGS Vox, Corbin

Organizations: US Army Corps of Engineers Nashville District Resource Manager, (606) 864-4163
    U.S. Forest Service, London Ranger District, at (606) 864-4163

Contacts/Outfitters: Sheltowee Trace Adventure Resort and Outfitters, 2001 Hwy 90, Corbin, KY 40701, (800) 541-7238 or (606) 526-7238, fun@ky-rafting.com, www.ky-rafting.com

Getting There

To Put-in/Take-out: From Corbin, take I-75 South at exit 29 for Cumberland Parkway/Ky. 1783/Ky. 770. Turn right at the exit, follow for 1.2 miles, and then turn left onto Ky. 312 East. In 0.7 mile, after crossing the Laurel River Bridge, turn left to follow the signs to the Laurel Bridge Recreation Area. The boat ramp is at the end of the road, with parking and picnic areas at the top of the hill. A set of wooden stairs connect the two.

River Overview

The US Army Corps of Engineers began work on the 282-foot-high Laurel River Dam in 1964. Its construction took 10 years, and in 1977, the lake was opened. The damming of the Laurel River created a deep reservoir that fluctuates between 5,600 and 6,100 acres, depending on the water level.

Following the channel from one end of the lake to the other is a distance of about 19 miles, but there are approximately 200 miles of shoreline, all of it protected public

Laurel River Lake with its steep rocky drop-offs is an excellent fishing lake for walleye and other fish species, which are enjoyed by humans and birds alike. CARRIE STAMBAUGH

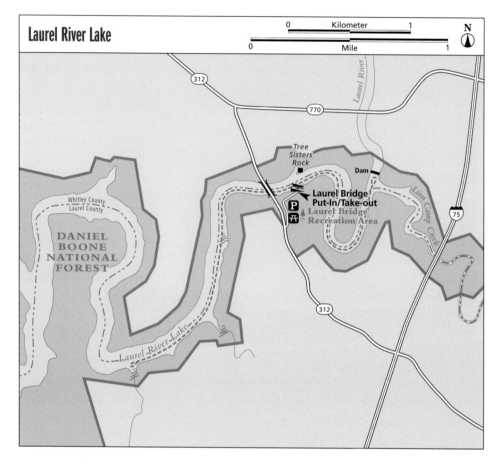

Laurel River Lake

land within the London District of the Daniel Boone National Forest. Laurel River Lake Dam is controlled by the Eastern Kentucky Power Cooperative. Below the dam, the Laurel River flows 2 miles to its confluence with Cumberland Lake. During release, it can offer some Class II to borderline Class IV whitewater, but when Cumberland Lake is at its typical summertime pool level, the rapids lie below flatwater.

There are two marinas on Laurel River Lake and four campgrounds. One campground, White Oak, is boat-in only, and it is located on the northern end of the lake. Dispersed camping is permitted along the shoreline, provided you pitch your tent at least 300 feet from the water's edge, which can be difficult to do in places due to the steep, hilly terrain.

Nine boat ramps provide access to a variety of water craft, including lots of motorized boats ranging in size from large houseboats to small runabouts and, of course, hand-powered craft. The lake holds plenty of black bass, crappie, bluegill, walleye, rainbow trout, and catfish.

The Paddle

This paddle begins and ends at the Laurel Bridge Boat Ramp. Directly across from the ramp, which is just 0.3 mile from the Ky. 312 bridge across the lake, is the Three Sisters Rock, a large boulder that is a popular place to cliff-jump, although it is prohibited.

From the launch, head left (west) toward the bridge and the main channel of the lake. Cross under the bridge, continuing to hug the shoreline as the lake bends around a corner. By mile 0.6, the launch and bridge are out of sight. The shoreline is heavily wooded, and large boulders dot the shoreline, and some rise out of the water several dozen feet from the shore.

Almost immediately upon making the turn from the bridge, we spotted a large bird of prey diving into the waters to grab a fish. It quickly flew out of sight over the treetops, its catch, the fish, still wriggling to escape its sharp talons.

The first of three small, hidden, wet-weather waterfalls can be heard at mile 0.94, along the southern bank (river left). These particular falls are located behind some large boulders that obscure the view from the main channel. Passing boaters on motorized crafts don't have a chance of hearing them or the ability to navigate to them through the narrow passage. This one is only for those in paddled crafts.

The second small waterfall can be heard at mile 1.4 and is again found along the rocky bank, tucked beneath heavy foliage. The third waterfall is at mile 1.8. Again, this one is obscured by thick foliage but is found in the back corner of a cove. This cove is somewhat wider, but again, it is protected by large, shallow rocks from larger boats. It does have a rocky point that makes a good place for landing and swimming. This is a good place to turn around and head back to the ramp. Just beyond this point, the river begins to widen significantly, resulting in more motorized boat traffic.

17 Rockcastle River

The Rockcastle River is a true gem, flowing freely through the Daniel Boone National Forest. A designated Kentucky Blue Water Trail and Kentucky Wild River, it is deserving of this title. This paddle explores the milder section of the river beginning just below the confluence of the Middle and South Forks and ending at the start of the whitewater section. It is an excellent and popular canoe camping run that offers great fishing and is appropriate for families.

Counties: Rockcastle, Laurel, Pulaski

Start: Wilderness Ford Road Launch (off U.S. 25)
N 37 17.680', W 84 13.102'

End: Old Howard Place Access (end of Bolthouse Ridge Road)
N 37 04.108 W 84.19.427

Length: 27.3 miles

Float Time: 12 hours, overnight

Difficulty: Moderate, due to length and several drops requiring maneuverability skills

Rapids: I, II+

River Type: Mountain river

Current: Moderate

River Gradient: 2.4 to 5.8 feet per mile

River Gauge: USGS Rockcastle at Billows. Minimum reading should be 220 cfs

Land Status: Public/Private

Nearest City/Town: Livingston

Boats Used: Canoe, Kayak, SUP

Season: Fall, winter, spring

Fees and permits: No

Maps: USGS Livingston, Bernstadt, Billows, Ano, Sawyer; Daniel Boone National Forest Map, South Section

Contact/Outfitter: Rockcastle Adventures Canoe Livery, 11137 Somerset Road, London, KY 40741; (606) 309-2976

Daniel Boone National Forest, London District, 761 S. Laurel Road, London, KY 40744; (606) 864-4163

Bee Rock Campground, (606) 865-4163

Rockcastle Campground, (606) 864-4163 or (606) 864-5225

Getting There

To Shuttle Point/Take-out: From Livingston to Old Howard Place. Note: A high clearance four-wheel drive vehicle is advised to access this take-out. This is a long shuttle of approximately 1 hour. From Livingston, travel south on U.S. 25 for 13 miles, and then continue onto Ky. 2041. In 2.1 miles, turn right to continue following Ky. 2041 for another 1.4 miles. Take a slight right onto Ky. 1956 after 0.4 mile, turn left onto Ky. 1035 (Pine Top Road) after 0.2 mile, and then turn right onto Ky. 80. Follow it for 17 miles, and then turn left onto Chimney Rock Church Road/County Road 1022. Follow it for 0.9 mile, and then turn left onto Squib-Ano Road. Turn left in 1 mile to continue on Squib-Ano Road. In another 1.7 miles, turn left onto Acorn-Ano Road. Follow it 0.3 mile to Bolthouse Ridge Road. Follow it until it ends next to the river in 4 miles.

The Rockcastle River appears tranquil in late fall in the Bee Rock area. PHOTO BY BEN CHILDERS PHOTOGRAPHY

To Put-in from Take-out: Retrace your path back toward Livingston. The put-in is on private land on the (east) side of U.S. 25 near the intersection of Mize-Sandhill Road, just 0.4 mile south of Livingston. It is visible from the roadway.

River Overview

The Rockcastle River drew its name from the cliffs that tower above the river, particularly in the gorge section known as the "Rockcastle Narrows," where 100-foot cliffs rise on either side of the waterway. It was discovered in 1750 by Dr. Thomas Walker and his exploring party and originally named the Lawless River, but it was renamed Rockcastle shortly after. The 54.8-mile river has two forks that join in Laurel County. Its south fork begins in and drains a portion of Clay County. The Middle Fork forms in southern Jackson County. The forks meet at the Jackson County line and flow south, forming the border of Rockcastle, Laurel, and Pulaski Counties, along the remainder of its length. A tributary of the Cumberland River, it now flows into the backwaters of Lake Cumberland. A 15.9-mile section from the Ky. 1956 bridge to its confluence with the slack water of Lake Cumberland is designated a Kentucky Wild River. It is one of the most remote paddles in Kentucky due to its location in the middle of the Daniel Boone National Forest.

This is one of the most popular paddles in the state because of its relative remoteness in the Daniel Boone National Forest. The Rockcastle is 60 to 80 feet wide for much

LOWER ROCKCASTLE: WHITEWATER SECTION

The lower Rockcastle River is one of Kentucky's most scenic and technical stretches of whitewater. The river is squeezed between 100-foot-high rock cliffs as it descends toward the Cumberland River.

The 5.6-mile stretch of water between the put-in at Old Howard Place and the take-out at Bee Rock Boat Ramp is one of the most challenging whitewater run in Kentucky. There are large boulders in and alongside the river for the entire stretch. The river twists and turns before plummeting over blind drops through this section, requiring excellent water reading and technical paddling skills. It also takes considerable time, as each rapid must be scouted. Boaters should always wear PFDs, and in this stretch, a helmet is advised.

A mile downstream of the Old Howard Place, the river tumbles over a sequence of steep ledges called "Stair Steps"; it is a Class II-III rapid. Paddlers are given a break over the next 2 miles with just Class II rapids before entering the final stretch of back-to-back technical rapids that include a set of Class IV ones at Beech Narrows. The start is marked by the river appearing to disappear into a rock garden, but it actually drops 4 feet after being squeezed between two large boulders. There is a mean keeper hydraulic below the drop, which has trapped and drowned numerous kayakers over the years. Past it, the current flows straight into a boulder. All kayakers are advised to scout this rapid, and most should portage it on the right. If you choose to run it, a rescue person should set up where they are certain they can reach a trapped boat on the first throw.

After another small stretch of calm water, the river again appears to come to a dead end; it doesn't. Beyond this tranquil pool, the river cuts hard right, pummels down a chute, and slams straight into another boulder. This is the beginning of the Lower Narrows, which is a three-quarter-mile stretch of continuous technical Class III-IV whitewater. Following the first rapid, there is a quick succession of four rapids as the river twists and falls. A number of large eddies provide some relief here and provide places to stop, exit kayaks, and then scramble over boulders to see what lies ahead.

Following the Narrows, there is one Class II and one Class III rapid, respectively. The first can trap logs. It is 1 mile to the take-out following the final Class III.

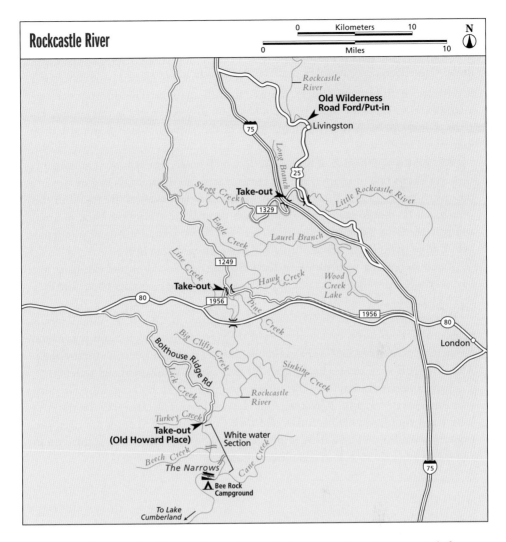

of its length. Large boulders and stunning rock formations line the river at different points throughout its length, and large boulders in the river can make for some interesting paddling. Mixed hardwood and evergreen forests blanket the rolling hillsides surrounding the river, which flows clear over a sand and rock bed. The banks vary in steepness along this stretch from gradual to high rock bluffs.

The paddle begins just south of Livingston, off U.S. 25, which parallels its winding course for the first 4.1 miles, until it crosses the river. A railroad on the other bank parallels this stretch too. As the river enters its first turn on this stretch, the Little Rockcastle River enters from the east at mile 4. The Rockcastle Trading Company is located on the western bank here.

After completing the first turn, the river makes a second one, and at mile 6, it crosses under the I-75 bridge. For those who want a small day trip, this is the place to take-out. The take-out is located on the west bank (river right) under the bridge and along Ky. 1329.

From here, the river is significantly windier with more drops making the paddling a little more exciting than the first stretch marked by longer, quieter pools. The water is very clear in this stretch, which can make the fishing for smallmouth and rock bass a little trickier. There are more large boulders and undercut rocks in this section. Ky. 1329 roughly parallels the river for 2 miles in this section, which is populated by homes and small farms.

Beyond the confluence of Skegg Creek, which enters from the west at mile 9.7, the river enters one of its most remote sections with no roads paralleling or crossing the river until Ky. 1956 at mile 16.6. A number of campsites can be found in this stretch, but be sure to take care to camp high enough away from the bank to avoid being flooded out, if rain is predicted. As the river curves southward, there are a number of drops that require maneuvering and make the paddling lively.

If you are ending your paddle at Ky. 1956, the take-out is on the east bank just beyond the bridge. The Rockcastle Adventure Canoe Livery is located here, and they do charge $5 to take-out here.

Beginning at Ky. 1956, the Rockcastle is designated as a Kentucky Wild River. It begins to pick up speed as the gradient of the river increases as it heads toward the lower, whitewater section! The next 10 miles is truly a gorgeous section for paddling. At mile 19, the river crosses beneath Ky. 80 after a long, relatively straight stretch.

Again, the river is remote in this stretch with no roads or homes nearby. The final take-out is located at mile 26.6 at the Old Howard Place. The take-out is on the west bank (river right), just before Turkey and Lick Creek combined enter the river, also from the west. Beyond here there is nowhere to take-out before the river turns mean and enters a 6-mile stretch of technical whitewater.

18 Big South Fork of the Cumberland River

The most popular paddle on the Big South Fork of the Cumberland River is a 4.8-mile stretch from the Blue Heron Mining Community to Yamacraw Landing, a lovely paddle that starts out with a lively Class II rapid. Downstream beyond Yamacraw, the river slows and widens as it heads toward becoming the depths of Lake Cumberland as it meanders through McCreary County. A paddle on the Big South Fork can easily be made into a 22-mile leisurely, multi-night camping trip that allows for plenty of time for fishing and exploring tributaries, including the Little South Fork of the Cumberland River, a Wild Kentucky River whose mouth is located just upriver from the final take-out described in this paddle.

County: McCreary
Start: Blue Heron Mining Community Ramp
N 36 40.086', W 84 32.765'
End: Yamacraw Landing: N 36 43.540', W 84 32.628'
   Alum Fork: N 36 45.837', W 84 32.849'
   Nevelsville: N 36 50.280', W 35.693'
Length: 4.8 to 22 miles
Float Time: 2.5 to 10 hours; overnight
Difficulty: Moderate, due to length some technical skills are required
Rapids: I, II
River Type: Narrow, rocky mountain stream to wide lake slack water
Current: Moderate to slow
River Gradient: 7-10 feet per mile, then none
River Gauge: USGS 03410500 Big South Fork of the Cumberland River near Stearns, Kentucky and USGS 03410210 Big South Fork of the Cumberland River at Leatherwood Ford, Tennessee.

The best flow rate for floating the river is between 200 and 500 cfs at Stearns. Between 500 and 1500 cfs at Stearns, the river is faster, and the floating is more interesting. Above 1500 cfs at Stearns, only experienced paddlers in kayaks and other closed boats should attempt this river. Beyond 3,000 cfs, there are extremely dangerous conditions.

Land Status: Public
Nearest Cities/Towns: Stearns, Whitley City
Boats Used: Canoe, Kayak
Season: Any
Fees or Permits: No fees or permits needed for day use. Backcountry camping permit required for overnight stays.
Maps: USGS Barthell, Nevelsville, Big South Fork National River and Recreation Area Map
Organizations: National Park Service, https://www.nps.gov/biso/index.htm
   American Whitewater, www.americanwhitewater.org/content/River/detail/id/1720/
Contacts/Outfitters: Sheltowee Trace Adventure Resort and Outfitters, 2001 Hwy 90, Corbin, KY 40701, (800) 541-7238 or (606) 526-7238, fun@ky-rafting.com, www.ky-rafting.com

Getting There

To Shuttle Point/Take-out (Nevelsville): From Whitley City take U.S. 27 north for 8 miles. Turn left onto Ky. 927 and follow for 8.8 miles. Parking is to the left before the end of the ramp. The alternate take-outs are also easily accessible from U.S. 27.

To Put-in from Take-out: Take Ky. 927 8.8 miles back to U.S. 27 south. Follow for 9.3 miles, then turn right onto Ky. 92 west and follow for 1.3 miles. Turn left onto Ky. 1651. In 0.5 mile turn right onto Ky. 741. In 0.7 mile turn right onto Ky. 742. In 5.9 miles arrive at the Blue Heron Mining Community. The boat ramp and parking are at the end of the road.

River Overview

The Big South Fork of the Cumberland River is created by the joining of Clear Fork and New Rivers of Tennessee. From this confluence, it flows through a narrow, towering crack in the southern end of the Cumberland Plateau as it heads for what is now the headwaters of Lake Cumberland.

The first 10 miles of the river, as it leaves Tennessee and flows to the restored mining community of Blue Heron, is a Wild Kentucky River. It is a wonder to behold both from above at the Devil's Jump Lookout and from the river itself.

This section of the river is remote—accessible from the Station Camp Put-in located in Oneida, Tennessee. It is 9 miles to the Kentucky–Tennessee border and another 10 miles to Blue Heron. It also requires (at least) one portage around the dangerous Class IV Devil's Jump rapid along with an overnight camping stay.

Luckily, the next 22 miles of river, beginning at the Blue Heron Mining Camp to the take-out at Ky. 927 near Nevelsville, is a much easier stretch of water to access and is also strikingly beautiful. This stretch of river is also much more suited for leisurely multiple overnight camping trips, as well as day trips of varying lengths.

The Paddle

On our paddle, the river was flowing at 650 cfs, up about 100 cfs from the night before due to some thunderstorms to the south in Tennessee. The water dropped quickly throughout the day, falling to below 500 cfs by the next afternoon. The water was as clear as the sky, however, and the rocky river bottom was visible at the put-in.

The first feature of the float is the same feature you passed below and marveled at on the way to the launch: the iron cantilevered bridge crossing the river at Blue Heron Mining Community. The 100-foot-high bridge carried special coal cars that opened in the bottom to dump coal into a large, main hopper. The tipple, which was modern in 1930 when it was first opened by the Stearns Coal and Lumber Company, could screen, separate, and then load into railcars at a rate of 400 tons of coal per hour.

The bridge today, with its striking ironwork coming to a decorative point in the center, perfectly frames the view downriver, which consists of colossal boulders sprinkled along the banks and in the middle of the river, which is hemmed between steep mountains thick with large hardwoods and evergreens.

At 0.9 mile, the first, and only, rapid of the paddle must be navigated. It's a Class II rapid that is easy enough for children to navigate on their first river runs at low levels. Beware the classic S curve rapid capable of upsetting a boat. Scout the rapid to plan

This bridge at Blue Heron once carried coal across the Big South Fork of the Cumberland River to a tipple. CARRIE STAMBAUGH

your path through the obstacle. There are a rocky point and large eddy on river right, upstream from the rapid and behind a large boulder that partially obstructs a view of it. This is a good spot to pull over and scout it—if only for practice.

On our run, the best line was to head toward river left to have time to adjust and be carried straight into the wave train, which heads directly toward the large rock on river right at the apex of the bend. A couple of hard strokes on the right will keep your craft far enough to river left to avoid the undercut rock; a little too hard and you will catch the small eddy at the bottom of the chute and maybe do a spin. (Just below the rapid, at mile 1.15, there is a second put-in on river right, so if this is too much excitement, you can skip it.)

The next landmark comes at mile 2.75 in the form of old bridge pylons that rise from the boulder field. Look for an old metal loop in a boulder on river left. The fishing in this stretch is spectacular. Many prized smallmouth bass have been caught in this stretch of river, which also holds a population of native walleye.

The river has flattened out and become wider, punctuated by the same gigantic boulders and more gravel bars, and small stretches of sunny sandbanks peek out beneath the towering trees. At mile 4.25, the Ky. 92 bridge comes into view.

BIG SOUTH FORK NATIONAL RIVER AND RECREATION AREA

The Big South Fork National River and Recreation Area was created by Congress in 1974 after some nudging from Kentucky and Tennessee lawmakers to preserve the stream and shoreline of the Big South Fork after the US Army Corps of Engineers floated the idea of building a dam at Devil's Jump.

In addition to the river, the 125,000-acre preserve managed by the National Park Service is also full of sandstone arches, creeks with abundant waterfalls, and the gorge itself. There are more than 130 miles of multi-use trails, including a portion of the long-distance hiking trail called The Sheltowee Trace, named for Daniel Boone, who was given the name Sheltowee meaning "Big Turtle," by Chief Blackfish of the Shawnee tribe. Beyond the BSFNRRA, the Daniel Boone National Forest's Stern District stretches north.

Despite the coal mining operations and the region being heavily logged, its natural beauty is still striking. The rocky hills have been reforested with hardwoods, evergreens, and mountain laurel. Vistas here are some of the most striking in Kentucky. The region is also still remote and wildlife abundant.

The abundance of natural arches is one of the largest draws for visitors to the area, but there are other reasons to visit as well. The restored Blue Heron mining town at the put-in for this paddle is one of the largest attractions. The riverside coal mining town was founded in 1937 by the Stearns Lumber Company, which shuttered the town in 1962 after becoming disappointed in its production. The automated mining exhibit created by the National Park Service, which uses first-person oral histories of life in the company town, is worth some time. Metal framed structures represent the various buildings that did not survive, but the coal tipple itself is authentic.

The Big South Fork Scenic Railway is another way to visit the gorge. The train runs from the town of Stearns, where the headquarters of the company were located, into the Gorge and stops at Blue Heron. A round-trip takes about 3 hours. For more information and a schedule of train excursions, visit www.bsfsry.com or call (800) 462-5664.

The Yamacraw Landing take-out is at mile 4.5, just past the bridge on river left. It can take quick paddlers less than 2 hours in a moderate current to reach the take-out here, while more leisurely types can stretch this float into a good half-day affair.

Beyond Yamacraw, the river increasingly widens, the current slows, and the banks become more heavily wooded with fewer gravel and sandbars.

At mile 7, the river begins the first of two consecutive bends to river right and then straightens out a bit as it heads past Alum Ford. As you go by, notice the rocky

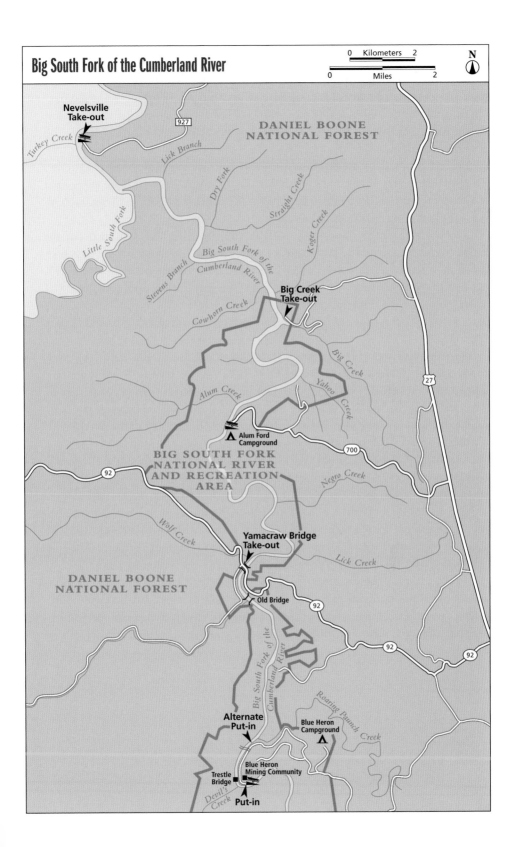

Big South Fork of the Cumberland River

0 Kilometers 2
0 Miles 2

N

927

DANIEL BOONE
NATIONAL FOREST

Turkey Creek

Nevelsville
Take-out

Lick Branch

Dry Fork

Straight Creek

Koger Creek

Little South Fork

Stevens Branch

Big South Fork of the
Cumberland River

Cowhorn Creek

Big Creek
Take-out

Big Creek

Alum Creek

Yahoo Creek

27

Alum Ford
Campground

BIG SOUTH FORK
NATIONAL RIVER
AND RECREATION
AREA

92

Negro Creek

700

Wolf Creek

Yamacraw Bridge
Take-out

Lick Creek

DANIEL BOONE
NATIONAL FOREST

Old Bridge

92

92

92

Big South Fork of the Cumberland River

Roaring Paunch

Alternate
Put-in

Blue Heron
Campground

Creek

Trestle
Bridge

Blue Heron
Mining Community

Devil's Creek

Put-in

shelf on the western bank that looks similar to a layered cake that's been sliced into portions. The river soon grows still wider, and the gravel bars and sandy banks disappear, as does the availability of flat, open riverside campsites. If you are doing a camping run and plan to continue down river toward Lake Cumberland, I'd advise you to stop at Alum Ford, which has six primitive sites and a concrete boat ramp. It's at mile 10.4 on river right.

Beyond Alum, there are precious few good camping spots for the next 11 miles. The paddling is also slower, and the number of powerboats increases with every mile as Lake Cumberland draws closer. The river is still alluring and the paddling interesting, and the fishing continues to be superb.

Yahoo Creek enters the river from river right at mile 11.4. On an overnight paddle, it's worth a detour to paddle as far up the creek as possible, land, and then hike the short distance to Yahoo Falls, which, at 80 feet, is the tallest waterfall in Kentucky.

The Big Creek take-out is located at mile 14.2, just upriver on the right from a water pump and is a third option for a long day paddle. Expect to paddle for at least 6 hours to reach this take-out on a day trip. Big Creek Road can also be hard to spot from U.S. 27.

Beyond Big Creek, the Big South Fork River and Recreation Area gives way to the Daniel Boone National Forest. From mile 14.2 to mile 20.7, campsites are limited to narrow rock ledges and clearings on sloping banks—fine if you camp in a hammock, not so much if you sleep in a tent. The shores are marked by stands of submerged trees, ghostly white figures marking the old boundaries of the river, before the slack waters of Lake Cumberland redrew them.

At mile 20.7, the Little South Fork of the Cumberland River joins the Big South Fork from river left. A narrow, rocky ridge on river left comes to a knife edge point where the two rivers meet.

The Little South Fork is a designated Wild Kentucky River but is harder to paddle because of its remoteness and seasonal nature and the absence of a USGS gauge to track water levels. It can typically be paddled from near Parmleysville to its confluence with the Big South Fork when the larger river is running high.

The last take-out before Lake Cumberland is in the center of a curve. The concrete ramp at the terminus of Ky. 927 is on river right at mile 21.8. You will notice several camps on river left with stairs and floating docks as you approach the ramp. It takes roughly 10 hours of continous paddling to make the trip from Blue Heron to the take-out here.

19 Ohio River

This paddle takes place downstream of the nation's eighth-busiest inland port that stretches from Charleston, West Virginia, to the Greenup Locks and Dam at Lloyd, Kentucky. Access on this part of the river is best from the Ohio side, but Kentucky "owns" the Ohio River to its historical highwater mark on the Ohio bank, so when one is standing on the "shore" of the Ohio side, they are technically still in Kentucky.

The river is wide—easily over a half-mile wide—and calm in this section, which is free from heavy industry along its banks. Farmland and a few communities dot the riverside on this stretch, which is quiet and can feel quite abandoned at times.

This stretch of water is of significant historical interest in that it was inhabited by the pre-Columbian, mound-building Hopewell culture, whose Adena people built an extensive system of earthworks that once stretched for miles on both sides of the river. By the time the first white settlers arrived, they found a thriving Shawnee settlement in the Ohio River Valley on the western side of the confluence of the Scioto and Ohio Rivers. It was called Lower Shawnee Town, and it is where the French first asserted their claims to the region, kicking off the French and Indian War.

Today, this stretch of river is bordered by farmlands and a few small towns downstream of Portsmouth and is noted for the ribbons of striking emerald-green hills along both sides of the river that rise steeply from the valley floor.

County: Greenup
Start: Doyle's Landing Boat Ramp, Portsmouth, Ohio
N 38 43.665', W 82 59.3310'
End: Shawnee State Park Marina, Friendship, Ohio
N 38 40.588', W 83 06.647'
Length: 8 miles
Float Time: 3 hours
Difficulty: Moderate (There can be a substantial current, debris, and plenty of motorized traffic on the river.)
Rapids: None
River Type: Wide, commercial waterway
Current: Slow to moderate
River Gradient: 0.3 feet per mile

River Gauge: http://www.lrh-wc.usace.army.mil/wm/?river/ohio - Maysville
Land Status: Private
Nearest Cities/Towns: Portsmouth, OH; West Portsmouth, OH; Friendship, OH; South Portsmouth, KY; Firebrick, KY; South Shore, KY
Boats Used: Canoe, Kayak, SUP
Season: Any
Fees or Permits: None
Maps: USGS Portsmouth, Friendship
Organizations: US Army Corps of Engineers, Huntington District
Contacts/Outfitters: Dragonfly Outdoor Adventures, 52B Treasure Cove Road, Greenup, KY 41144, (606) 465-0306; dragonflyoutdoor adventures.com

Getting There

To Shuttle Point/Take-out: Take U.S. 52 west from Portsmouth approximately 9.5 miles to the Shawnee State Park Marina. Turn left on the park road then make an

The "beautiful river" flows calmly between wide river valleys and wooded hills as it runs past eastern Ohio and Kentucky. CARRIE STAMBAUGH

MURALS AT PORTSMOUTH, OHIO

The floodwall at Portsmouth, Ohio, is home to a 2,000-foot-long series of murals depicting the more than 2,000 years of local history. From the river, boaters only get a glimpse of the treasures painted on the wall in the large patriotically colored printing of "Portsmouth, Ohio" that announces the town to river arrivals, along with stars bearing the names of its most notable citizens.

Located on the east side of the mouth of the Scioto River, Portsmouth was founded in 1803 and survives today because it is located on the highest ground in the area. The Ohio and Scioto Rivers have repeatedly flooded throughout history, wiping out both Native American and white-settled towns along the lower shores.

Strategically located on the river where railroad lines and the southern end of the Ohio and Erie Canal all converged, the city became an important industrial hub by the early twentieth century.

The massive floodwall that hides Portsmouth from the river was mostly constructed in the 1940s following the devastating flood of 1937. Major floods also took place in 1884 and 1913. The floodwalls are now credited with preventing flooding in 1964, 1997, and, most recently, 2018.

By the end of the 1980s, the city was struggling with the same economic decline caused by the erosion of its manufacturing base that was occurring throughout the Rust Belt. At that time, a group of citizens came together to create the public work of art in an effort to attract visitors to the historic city.

Mural artist Robert Dafford was hired in 1993 to begin painting the first murals. He hired local artist Herb Roe to assist him. To date, there are sixty 20-foot-long murals depicting important citizens, sporting events, and the earliest Native Americans to inhabit the area.

immediate right to take the road to the marina and boat ramps. There are three ramps and ample parking for large vehicles beyond the ramps.

To Put-in from Take-out: From the marina, take U.S. 52 east to Portsmouth. In 8.4 miles, turn right onto Offnere Street. Follow Offnere street for 0.8 mile. Then take a right to follow the one-way park road around to the boat ramps. Parking is available in several parking lots.

River Overview

The mighty Ohio River defines the northern border of Kentucky from its confluence with the Big Sandy River at Catlettsburg, Kentucky, until it empties into the

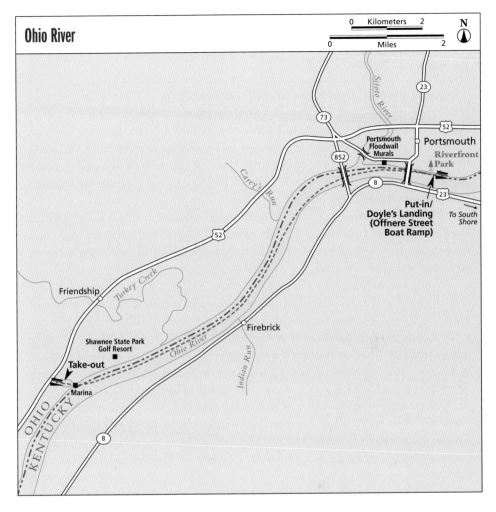

Ohio River

0 Kilometers 2
0 Miles 2
N

Scioto River

23

73

52

Portsmouth
Floodwall
Murals

Portsmouth

852

**Riverfront
Park**

Carey's Run

8

23

**Put-in/
Doyle's Landing
(Offnere Street
Boat Ramp)**

*To South
Shore*

52

Friendship

Turkey Creek

Firebrick

Shawnee State Park
Golf Resort

Ohio River

Indian Run

Take-out

Marina

OHIO
KENTUCKY

8

Mississippi River just north of Wickliffe, Kentucky. The Ohio River is 981 miles long and begins in Pittsburgh, Pennsylvania, where the Monongahela and Allegheny Rivers meet and ends at Cairo, Illinois, where it is the single largest tributary of the Mississippi River. The Ohio River drains fifteen states, an area of more than 189,000 square miles, and provides drinking water to more than three million Americans.

The Ohio River played a major role in Native American life and in the settlement and early economic development of the United States. It remains a vital transportation corridor to this day, with barges hauling millions of tons of freight up and down the river annually.

Locks and dams began being built along the Ohio River as early as the 1830s, when a canal was built to bypass the Falls of the Ohio at Louisville, and by the 1950s, there were nineteen locks and dams on the river, which the US Army Corps of Engineers now manage. These man-made structures have broken the river into twenty-one pools of slow-moving and nearly constantly navigable waterways.

The Paddle

The paddle begins at Doyle's Landing in Portsmouth, Ohio, a public boat ramp area inside the city's floodwall, just upstream from the main downtown area. Upon entering the water, head downstream in a southwesterly direction, hugging the northern bank of the river toward the pair of bridges that connect Kentucky and Ohio along this stretch of river. The first bridge, at 0.5 mile, is the new cable-stay US Grant Bridge, which carries U.S. 23 across the river. The Shawnee Boat Club and a second boat ramp are located here beneath the bridge.

The city of Portsmouth rises from behind the floodwall, which is painted with a large mural on the river facing side. At mile 1.3, the Scioto River enters the Ohio from the north. On the Kentucky side of the river, a high, narrow ridgetop comes to an abrupt end above the river.

At mile 1.6, paddle under the Carl D. Perkins Bridge, a steel cantilever structure that carries U.S. 23 truck route and Ohio 852 across the river to the intersection of Ky. 8.

The river widens significantly downstream of the Scioto and begins to curve more toward the south as it passes the small community of South Portsmouth, Kentucky. The banks are wooded, and a few houses can be seen above the river, which alternates between sand, gravel, and grass beds along its banks.

At the 4-mile mark, a number of homes that comprise the settlement of Firebrick come into view on the Kentucky side, and by mile 4.5, the river curves to the north and disappears briefly from view behind high green hills. It was in this stretch I noted a juvenile bald eagle flying along the bank, its white tail feathers standing out in the sunshine.

At mile 6.1, Turkey Creek enters the Ohio River from the north. Again, downstream, the river seems to disappear as it curves again toward the south. Stay close to the northern bank of the river.

At mile 7.8, a sign for the Shawnee State Marina appears at the mouth of the cove, which can be hard to spot because of thick vegetation. The Shawnee State Park Golf Course is not visible from the river, behind a ribbon of hardwoods.

Enter the cove and bear left, passing by a trio of boat docks, to head to the back of the cove and a trio of cement boat ramps at mile 8.

20 Kincaid Lake

This is an out-and-back loop paddle using the main channel of the lake. It also explores the headwaters of the lake as well as a side tributary. The paddle can be completed in as few as 3 hours, but an angler could easily spend an entire day battling bass.

County: Pendleton
Start and End: Kincaid Lake Boat Ramp
N 38 43.413', W 84 17.439'
Length: 6.6 miles
Float Time: 3 hours
Difficulty: Easy
Rapids: None
River Type: Lake
Current: Slow
River Gradient: None
River Gauge: None
Land Status: Public/private

Nearest City/Town: Falmouth
Boats Used: Canoe, Kayak, SUP
Season: Any
Map: USGS Falmouth, Kincaid Lake State Park
Fees and Permits: None
Contact/Outfitter: Kincaid Lake State Park, 565 Kincaid Park Road, Falmouth, KY 41040, (859) 654-3531, Parks.ky.gov/parks/recreationparks/Kincaid-lake/index.html
Thaxton's Canoe, (859) 472-2000; www.gopaddling.com

Getting There

To Put-in/Take-out: From Falmouth, Kentucky, at the intersection of U.S. 27 North and Main Street, turn onto Ky. 22/Main Street heading north through town for 1.3 miles. Turn left onto Ky. 159, following it 3.5 miles to Kincaid Lake State Park on the right. After entering the park, travel a half a mile to the boat ramp.

Lake Overview

Kinkaid Lake is a 189-acre impound of Kincaid Creek in Pendleton County. Most of the lake lies within the boundaries of Kincaid Lake State Park. The tailwaters of the lake enter the Licking River downstream of Falmouth. The south and main branches of the Licking River come together at Falmouth before flowing 39 miles and then emptying into the Ohio River at Cincinnati, Ohio.

Kinkaid Lake was created entirely for recreation. In fact, the citizens of Pendleton and surrounding counties raised the funds to purchase the land to create the lake and park, which they then donated to the state. The park was created in 1958, and work began on clearing the land for the lake, but construction on the dam did not start until 1961. Kincaid Lake State Park and the lake itself opened to the public in 1963.

Today, the park encompasses 850 acres and includes a campground, golf course, amphitheater, gift shop, grocery store, boat ramp, and a thirty-eight-slip marina with boat rentals. Swimming is no longer allowed in the lake; instead, a public pool is located lakeside.

Kincaid Lake offers quiet family paddling in Pendleton County. Carrie Stambaugh

The lake is noted for its fishing. Anglers can catch bass, crappie, bluegill, and catfish. The state park boasts that the lake produces more bass per acre than any other lake in Kentucky!

The Paddle

The paddle begins and ends at Kincaid Lake boat ramp, next to the earthen dam. The ramp is a simple concrete ramp with a small courtesy dock nearby.

Begin by heading east down the main channel of the lake. In 0.36 mile, a small cove on the right (south) holds the lakes small marina. Continue heading east, and in 0.86 mile, the public pool is located above the lake on the southern shore. There is a set of stairs leading down to what was once a public beach. In my childhood, I spent many summers swimming here during family camping trips.

Across the lake, there are private homes and boat docks along the gently sloping wooded banks. The park itself is entirely on the southern side of the shoreline.

Continuing to hug the southern bank, and then follow the lake eastward as it curves first north and then south around a peninsula of land that holds the state park campgrounds. In 1.3 miles, campsites come into view, again to the south. The lake has

Kincaid Lake

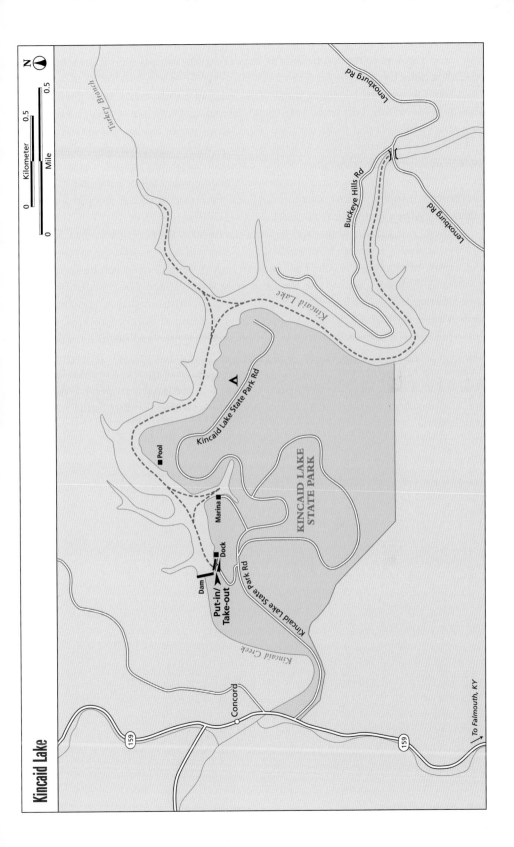

now curved around to the south. Directly across from the campground is the mouth of Turkey Branch Creek.

Along the wooded lakeshore, there is evidence of beaver, and a large flock of Canada geese calls the lake home year-round. They particularly like to occupy a narrow gravel peninsula that sticks out from the eastern shore as the lake narrows at the end of the park and curves again to head in a more east-west flow. Waterfowl of varying types can be spotted depending on the seasons, but large blue heron is a common site, as they were on my paddle. I also spotted a mature bald eagle soaring above the lakeshore on a sunny autumn afternoon. A local fisherman spotted it too and commented on what a rare sight it was indeed!

A number of summer homes and cottages dot the now steeper bank to the north and west at mile 2.3. You are now paddling upstream in Kincaid Creek, the shallower and narrow tributary to the lake. The southern bank is dominated by pasture land.

At mile 2.95, you pass beneath the Lenoxburg Road Bridge. The creek has narrowed further, and it is still navigable, but this is a good turnaround spot. Head back toward the main channel, at mile 4.5, reaching the mouth of Turkey Creek, which enters from the northeast. The tributary holds private homes and docks but offers excellent cover for bass fishing. In the fall and early spring, it is quiet. A half mile into the creek, it narrows significantly. Turn around and head back to the main lake, making a turn to the right (or west) when you reach the channel at mile 5.4. Follow the northern shore, cutting across the lake just before reaching the dock at the ramp at mile 6.6.

21 Licking River

This short paddle on the Licking River is a way to see the skyline of Cincinnati, Ohio, from another angle. Like most urban paddles, it is all about experiencing the juxtaposition of nature versus human development.

Counties: Campbell, Kenton
Start: Frederick's Landing Park, City of Wilder, Kentucky
N 39 03.034', W 84 29.584'
End: General James Taylor Park, Newport, Kentucky
N 39 05.284', W 84 30.260'
Length: 3.5 miles
Float Time: 1.5 hours
Difficulty Rating: Moderate
Rapids: None
River Type: Wide, urban river
Current: Slow
River Gradient: 1 foot per mile

River Gauge: USGS 03253500 Licking River at Catawba, KY. The minimum reading should be 120 cfs
Land Status: Public/private
Nearest City/Town: Wilder, Newport, Covington
Boats Used: Canoe, Kayak, SUP
Season: Any
Fees or Permits: It costs $2 to park at Frederick's Landing
Maps: USGS Covington, Newport
Contacts/Outfitters: Thaxton's Canoe and Paddler's Inn, 33 Hornbeek Road, Butler, KY, (859) 472-2000, gopaddling.com, info@gopaddling.com

Getting There

To Shuttle Point/Take-out: General James Taylor Park is located at the confluence of the Ohio River and Licking River in downtown Newport. The easiest way to reach the take-out is to access Riverboat Row through the floodwall at the entrance to Newport on the Levy, turn left, and drive to its end in the park.

If the access there is closed, Riverboat Row can also be accessed from Third Street via Columbia Street. Heading west toward Covington on Third Street, bear right through the traffic circle, and then make a right onto Columbia Street. In 0.1 mile, it passes through the floodwall and becomes Riverboat Row. Turn left and find parking on the right.

To Put-in from Take-out: It is 3.7 miles to the put-in at Frederick's Landing in Wilder from the take-out. Retrace your route back to Third Street. At the traffic circle, take the second exit onto Chestnut Way. It soon becomes Lowell Street, then Ky. 9. In 3.2 miles, Frederick's Landing Park will be on the right. Follow the signs to the boat ramp and parking.

River Overview

The Licking River is a wide urban river as it approaches the Ohio River. It separates the cities of Covington and Newport, which are located on the west and east sides

A fish-eye view of the Cincinnati skyline is the highlight of this urban paddle.
CARRIE STAMBAUGH

of the river, in Kenton and Campbell Counties, respectively. The modern cities are linked, of course, by two railroad and two vehicular and pedestrian bridges.

Many of the first settlers came to the area via the Ohio River, including Native Americans, early French voyageurs, and, later, the pioneers who settled it permanently beginning in 1788.

The modern metropolis of the Greater Cincinnati Area has a population of 2.1 million that reside in Ohio, Kentucky, and Indiana.

The Paddle

The destination of this paddle is the confluence of the Licking and Ohio Rivers. The skyline of the cities of Cincinnati, Ohio, which includes that of Newport and Covington, Kentucky, on the southern bank of the Ohio River, is among the prettiest in the country, in my opinion. I'm a native of Cincinnati, and no matter what mode of transportation you are using, when the glittering steel and glass skyline appears between lush, green hills above the river, it is a sight to behold. This is America's Queen City.

In my opinion, the easiest take-out is in Newport, Kentucky, but several other options would be suitable in both Ohio and Kentucky, depending on the season, river conditions, and what is happening in the area that day.

There is wildlife along the river: deer, a variety of ducks, the ubiquitous Canada goose, jumping and dead fish, circling vultures looking for the dead fish, along with lots of turtles plopping off logs and into the water. Stretches of the Licking are quiet, and then suddenly it can be interrupted by a thunderous scraping and shrieking of metal as a load of scrap is loaded onto a river barge.

Barge traffic on the Licking River can be very quiet on weekends and evenings when the Ohio is busy with other, faster watercraft. I'd avoid this paddle during the busy summer boating holidays, including Labor Day.

The put-in for this paddle is on Route 9 at Frederick's Landing. The park has ample parking and trailer space, and there is a $2 fee for parking. The launch has a nice floating dock and a concrete ramp with a turnaround.

It is 3.4 miles from the put-in to the Ohio River and 3.1 miles to the boat ramp at Newport's General James Taylor Park across the Licking River from Covington's historical district. It can be a quick paddle when the river is up, but it can also be a nice, leisurely evening trip for the kayak fisherman.

The first things you notice on the paddle are the number and variety of bridges that connect the cities of Newport and Covington. These are relics from the economies and culture of the past. Today, the bridges at 11th Street and 4th Streets connect the cities along with the I-275 loop.

However, the first bridge just past the put-in is an unused rail bridge. The second, at mile 2, is well used, as evidenced by how busy River Metals Recycling is along the eastern (river right) shore. The 11th Street Bridge is next at mile 2.2.

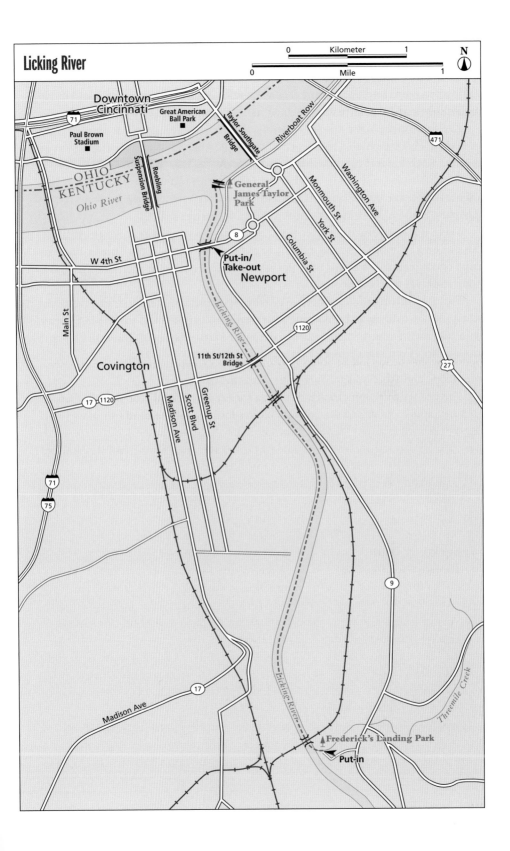

Just past mile 2, the tops of Cincinnati's tallest buildings, including the Proctor and Gamble Towers and the Carew Tower, begin to come into view above the trees. As you paddle, more landmarks come into view until, finally, Cincinnati's Great American Ball Park and the Serpentine Wall come into view across the wide river.

The final bridge is the 4th Street Bridge at mile 3.1 The take-out is on river right beneath it. There are both a concrete ramp and a floating dock. The Cincinnati Junior Rowing Club has its boathouse here above the river.

Pass the bridge and paddle another 0.3 mile to the confluence of the river to get a sense of the size of the Ohio River and the soaring buildings overlooking it. The Roebling Suspension Bridge dominates the view to river left.

There is a large beach on river right, at the mouth of the Ohio River. At times, this can be a solid beach for taking-out or just a sticky pile of mud. I prefer the boat ramp over potentially losing a shoe in river muck and having to walk through goose poop and river trash barefoot.

This is an urban paddle, so beware of where you park your car and who is around when you are loading and unloading your gear. This park has had trouble in the past with homeless, break-ins, and other undesirable human behavior. But don't let that dissuade you from seeing the city from a different angle!

Central Kentucky

22 Kentucky River / Boone Creek

This paddle explores a part of the Kentucky River Palisades starting from historic Fort Boonesborough. It also includes a side trip into Boone Creek, where the narrow creek flows between stunningly high cliffs. The paddle can easily be extended to include a longer trip further into the Palisades but requires an out-and-back paddle at the end.

Counties: Madison, Clark, Fayetteville
Start: Fort Boonesborough State Park Boat Ramp
N 37 54.092', W 84 15.978'
End: Clays Ferry Boat Ramp (beside Proud Mary BBQ, 9097 Old Richmond Road, Lexington, KY)
N 37 53.202', W 84 20.343'
Distance: 6.7 miles
Float Time: 4 hours
Difficulty: Moderate
Rapids: None
River Type: Flood-controlled, winding river between steep, wooded cliffs
Current: Moderate
River Gradient: 1 foot per mile
River Gauge: USGS Kentucky River at Lock 10/Winchester. The minimum reading should be 800 cfs.

Land Status: Private
Nearest Cities/Towns: Lexington, Nicholasville, Richmond, Winchester
Boats Used: Canoe, Kayak, SUP
Season: Any
Fees or Permits: None
Maps: USGS Ford
Contacts/Outfitters: Boone Creek Outdoors, 8291 Old Richmond Road, Lexington, KY 40515, (859) 494-7539, boonecreekoutdoors.com
   SUP Kentucky, 9070 Old Richmond Road (in the parking lot of Proud Mary BBQ), (859) 893-9342, SUPKentucky.com
   Three Trees Canoe and Kayak, 300 Athens-Boonesboro Road, Winchester, KY, (859) 749-3227

Getting There

To Shuttle Point/Take-out: From Lexington, travel south on I-75 to exit 99 for Old Richmond Road / U.S. 25/U.S. 421 North toward Clays Ferry. Turn right onto Old Richmond Road. Proud Mary BBQ is on the right in 1 mile. The boat ramp is to the west of the restaurant.

To Put-in from Take-out: From the parking lot of Proud Mary's, head north on Ky. 2328 (Old Richmond Road) for 1.7 miles, crossing the river. Turn left onto U.S. 25/U.S. 421 North. Follow it for 0.3 mile, and then continue straight onto Igo Road. In a half mile, turn left onto Simpson Lane. In 3.1 miles, turn right onto Combs Ferry Road. In 0.2 mile, turn left onto Ky. 627 North. In 1.2 miles, turn right onto Ky. 388. In 0.3 mile, turn right, and follow that to the end of the road and boat ramp.

The Kentucky River at historic Clays Ferry PROSPER MEDIA

River Overview

The Kentucky River Palisades is a 100-mile section of river from Clay's Ferry in Madison County to Frankfort in Franklin County that passes through 450-million-year-old limestone cliffs that soar to 400 feet. Specifically, the cliff is Lexington limestone—composed of thin limestone and interbedded shale.

The forest along this stretch of river is the largest remaining in the inner Bluegrass region and supports the unique ecosystem of the area, which also consists of steep gorges and an intricate cave system fed by springs. The forest itself is comprised of beech and yellow poplars, which grow on the terraces and banks of the river's tributaries. The steep slopes and higher elevations contain blue ash, chinquapin oak, sugar maple, rock elm, yellowwood, and yellow buckeye.

The Paddle

The Kentucky River below Beattyville where its forks come together is shared by paddled and motorized craft. It remains scenic, however, especially in this stretch at the beginning of the Palisades portion.

Launching from Fort Boonesborough State Park, the bridge carrying Ky. 627 (Boonesborough Road) over the river is 0.3 mile downriver. Upon passing it, on river left is the Boonsboro Quarry. At mile 0.7 is the Three Trees Canoe and Kayak Rental on river right just as it begins to make its curve to the west.

The Palisades soar 400 feet above the Kentucky River. CARRIE STAMBAUGH

Kentucky River / Boone Creek

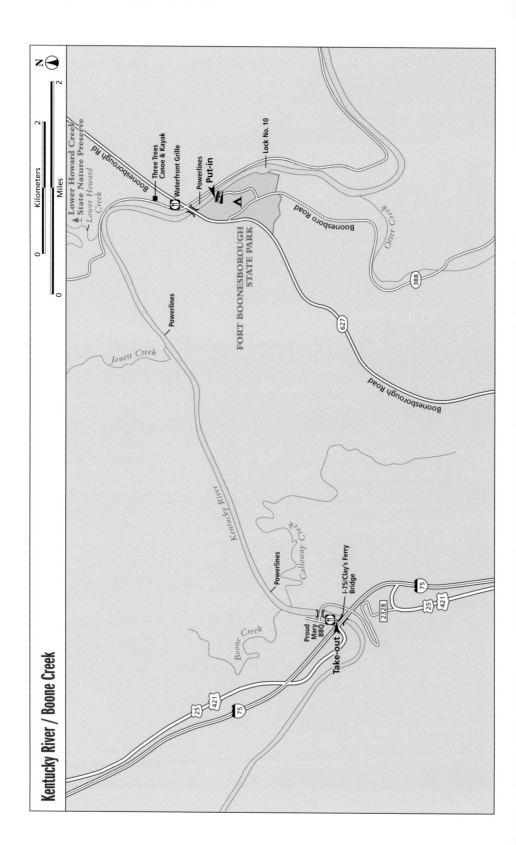

At mile 1.3, the river enters a long, straight stretch, and Lower Howard Creek enters from the north (river right). The famous Halls Along the River restaurant is located up this stream.

From here, the landscape begins to change as first the southern bank and then the northern bank become high cliff walls. This is the beginning of the Palisades.

At mile 2.5, Jouett Creek also enters from the north, just past a set of power lines. From here to Boone Creek, there are few signs of civilization, and only trees are visible above the river.

At mile 5.3, you reach the mouths of Boone Creek to the north and Calloway Creek to the south. Boone Creek is worth a side trip. Immediately upon entering the narrow waterway, notice the steep cliffs that mark its banks. Boone Creek has its own set of "palisades" created by the same limestone rock in what is referred to as Boone Creek Gorge.

The most pristine waterway in Fayette County, the creek is striking and windy. When water from the Kentucky backs up into the creek, it is possible to paddle up into the gorge section, which, fortunately, is located near the end of the creek. This is not possible when the waterway is flowing swiftly after rains.

On my paddle, I made it just shy of a mile into the creek before shallow water and a logjam forced me to turn around. Retracing my path, I reached the Kentucky River at mile 6.3, and I again headed downstream. The bridges that carry Ky. 2328 /U.S. 25 and I-75 are visible in the distance. The U.S. 25 Bridge is the smaller of the two, and it is reached at mile 6.7. The take-out is another tenth of a mile further on the right. This is the historic Clays Ferry Crossing.

It is possible to extend the trip from here further into the Palisades. In fact, some of the most striking of the cliffs are located in the next stretch of river, which is remote. Unfortunately, the next take-out is 12 miles further downriver, and the shuttle between the two can take more than 90 minutes!

Past Clays Ferry, the river makes a sharp turn and heads north for a stretch. Bulls Head Cliff is visible on the southwestern shore, and 2 miles downriver is the cliff known as Palisades. The cliff and its unique ecosystem are preserved as Floracliff State Nature Preserve. After this, the river makes another turn to the south, passing Raven Run Nature Preserve, 3.5 miles from Clay's Ferry.

23 Elkhorn Creek

This 7.6-mile stretch of water is one of Kentucky's most well-known and well-used whitewater paddles in the heart of Kentucky's Bluegrass region. It is known as the Gorge Section of Elkhorn Creek because it passes between soaring limestone bluffs that create a set of mini-palisades surrounded by pastoral countryside.

County: Franklin
Start: Forks of the Elkhorn Bridge Kayak Put-in / 3894 Georgetown Road
N 38 12.902', W 84 47.917'
End: Knights Bridge / Peak's Mill Road (Ky. 1900), American Whitewater (AW Acres) Take-out
N 38 16.077', W 84 48.927'
Distance: 7.6 miles
Float Time: 3 hours
Difficulty: Moderate to difficult; whitewater paddling skills required
Rapids: I, II (III)
River Type: Rocky, pastoral stream with whitewater
Current: Moderate to swift
River Gradient: 10 feet per mile
River Gauge: USGS 3289500 Elkhorn Creek at Knights Bridge. The best flows for beginners and intermediate paddlers are between 300 and 600 cfs. Flows of 600 cfs up to 3,000 cfs are considered to be prime levels for whitewater kayaking, but flows above 1,500 are recommended for experienced paddlers only.
Land Status: Private
Nearest City/Town: Frankfort
Boats Used: Kayak
Season: Late fall to early summer
Fees or Permits: Elkhorn Campground charges $3 to park and launch from the Forks of the Elkhorn Bridge
Maps: USGS East Frankfort, Switzer
Organizations: Bluegrass Wildwater Association, bluegrasswildwater.org
AmericanWhitewater.org
Contacts/Outfitters: Canoe Kentucky, 1-(888)-CANOEKY
Elkhorn Creek Campground, 165 North Scruggs Lane, Frankfort, KY 40601, (502) 695-9154, elkhorncampground.com

Getting There

To Shuttle Point/Take-out: From Frankfort, take U.S. 127 North to Ky. 1900. Turn right onto Ky. 1900, and follow it for 4.4 miles to the American Whitewater Elkhorn Acres River Access on the left before the roadway crosses the river.

To Put-in: From the parking lot, turn right and follow Ky. 1900 for 2.2 miles. Turn left onto Steadmantown Lane, traveling 1.9 miles before turning left to stay on the roadway. Continue for another 1.1 miles, then turn left onto East Main Street. In 0.3 miles, continue onto U.S.-460 E / Georgetown Road. Follow it for 0.9 mile, and then turn right onto North Scruggs Lane just after crossing over South Elkhorn Creek. The put-in is immediately to the right beneath the bridge.

Elkhorn Creek is one of the most famous whitewater paddles in Kentucky with views of distilleries, pastoral Central Kentucky, and soaring limestone cliffs. CARRIE STAMBAUGH

River Overview

Elkhorn Creek is formed from the merger of North Elkhorn Creek and South Elkhorn Creek, which occurs just west of Frankfort at the Forks of the Elkhorn. The river's width fluctuates from about 35 feet wide in this section to 90 feet. Occasional logjams and low branches, in addition to a dangerous low head dam, are the only dangers to navigation.

The Paddle

The launch is under the bridge just as the streams converge. Almost immediately, paddlers will encounter their first set of rapids, the second of which is formed by the remains of an old low head dam arching across the river. The wave it forms is named Church Wave, and it is located just 0.2 mile into the paddle. (At high levels, this becomes a "play spot" for boaters.)

The river curves gradually to the right. Look for a Jim Beam Bourbon Distillery on the right at 0.7 mile and a set of bridges leading to it. Be sure to keep to river left when rounding the bend in the creek and passing under the bridges. Be prepared to

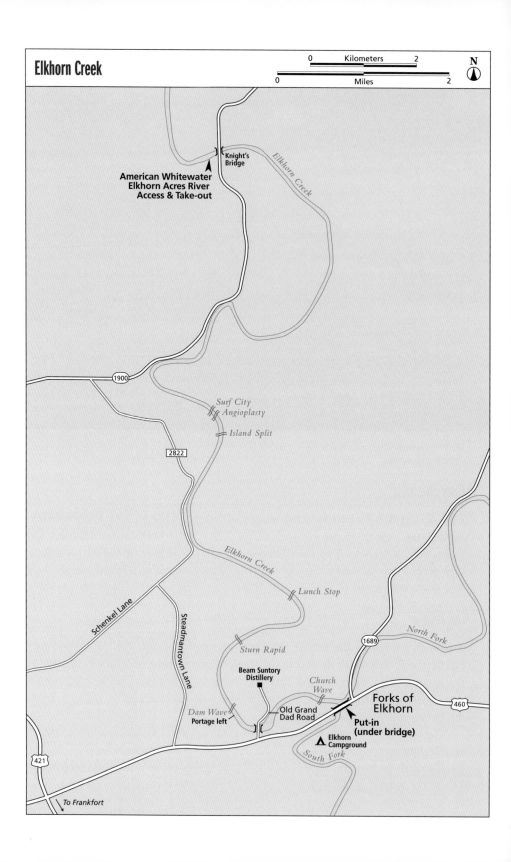

land just upstream from the low head dam. The take-out is very small and hard to see—it is only large enough for one or two boats.

The dam is extremely dangerous, and the portage around it can be very hazardous at water levels above 3,000 cfs. The portage requires carrying the boat down a stepped rock cliff.

Be careful to launch far enough downstream to avoid being sucked back into the reverse current of the dam. This dam is known as a "drowning machine" among local paddlers, as a number of fatal and near-fatal drownings have occurred here.

Removal of the dam has long been supported by the Bluegrass Wildwater Association and a number of other stakeholders. It did seem to be gaining momentum at one time but stalled. Following the drowning of an experienced kayaker in 2018, there is renewed pressure on local authorities to take action.

Be prepared to paddle hard to ferry across the current to mid-river to line up for the first big rapid of the float, Dam Rapid, which lies just downstream at mile 0.9.

The next rapid, S-Curve, comes at mile 1.5 and is noted for its diagonal wave, which seems to be at its maximum height when the river is flowing between 1,500 and 2,000 cfs.

This section is especially scenic as the river passes through soaring limestone cliffs. A wave to river right can create some fun lateral waves to play in and occurs at mile 2. It is called "Lunch Spot" because the bank is easily accessible here and a good place to stop for lunch.

At mile 3.6, the river splits around a long island. Stay to river right, but be careful since there can often be a logjam along the right bank, which I've seen flip more than one kayaker.

Next is a hydraulic hole named "Angioplasty," which is a solid Class II and sometimes a Class III at higher levels. It is at mile 3.7.

Immediately following it at mile 3.8 is "Surf City," a Class I rapid comprised of a series of fun waves.

From there, the Elkhorn remains relatively calm but scenic, and the paddling is interesting with constant shoals and riffles. The take-out is just past Knight's Bridge, which carries Peak's Mill Road (Ky. 1900) over the river on the left at mile 7.6.

24 North Elkhorn Creek

North Elkhorn Creek winds its way through the city of Georgetown. The smart citizens of the town have set aside the land inside a horseshoe bend in the heart of the city as a public park. It makes for a convenient, refreshing float trip in the heat of summer days, as well as a pleasant little paddle during most of the year.

In 2018, the City of Georgetown and Scott County tourism began an organized river float in early June. It enjoyed instant success. This paddle is the stretch of river used in the float and can easily be extended for a longer day trip.

Dry Run Creek joins North Elkhorn at almost the midway point of the float and is an interesting little side paddle as it heads toward Bi-Water Farm and Greenhouse, a family-owned and -operated farm known for its farmers market, live plants, and its Autumnfest.

County: Scott

Start: Peninsula Park, Georgetown
N 38 13.473', W 84 33.746'

End: Cardome Park, Peninsula Park, Georgetown
N 38 13.255', W 84 33.746'

Distance: 1.2 miles

Float Time: 2 hours

Difficulty: Easy. Perfect for families with small children.

Rapids: None

River Type: Suburban stream

Current: Slow to moderate

River Gradient: 4 feet per mile

River Gauge: USGS 3288100 North Elkhorn Creek near Georgetown, KY. Best flows are between 75 to 250 cfs.

Land Status: Public/private

Nearest City/Town: Georgetown

Boats Used: Canoe, Kayak, SUP

Season: All

Fees or Permits: No fees or permits are required

Maps: USGS Georgetown

Contacts/Outfitters: Canoe Kentucky, 1-(888)-CANOEKY

Getting There

To Shuttle Point/Take-out: Peninsula Park is located in the heart of Georgetown just off U.S. 25, which parallels it for its entire length. From U.S. 25, turn onto Payne Street, and then make an almost immediate left into the park. The boat ramp is located less than a tenth of a mile down the road.

To Put-in from Take-out: Travel the park road for 0.4 miles to reach the point where the road loops back toward the entrance to the park. Walk across the lawn here to put-in from the gently sloping bank.

River Overview

North Elkhorn Creek gathers itself in northeastern Fayette County and continues its journey northwest to Georgetown in Scott County. The creek is shallow with rock

The Elkhorn flows through Central Kentucky's bourbon distilling region. CARL STAMBAUGH

bars and beds of water willow and is noted for its smallmouth fishing. As it passes through Georgetown, several low head dams create a series of pools.

After Georgetown, the creek continues its westward course, flowing through a place known as the Great Crossing, named for the herds of buffalo (American bison) that once crossed the river here. West of Frankfort, it joins South Elkhorn Creek at the community of Forks of the Elkhorn. The confluence is the beginning of another, more-active paddle that is one of Kentucky's most well-known and beloved whitewater runs. Elkhorn Creek eventually flows into the Kentucky River outside of Frankfort.

The Paddle

This paddle starts on the eastern edge of the horseshoe around Georgetown's Peninsula Park along the south bank of the creek.

The river flows north then south around Peninsula Park. Dry Creek comes in at almost the apex of the bend from the north, at mile 0.4 from the put-in.

The banks are gentle, less than 2 or 3 feet high in places. On river left, the shore is well-maintained with grass that comes up almost to the edge of the banks. Large

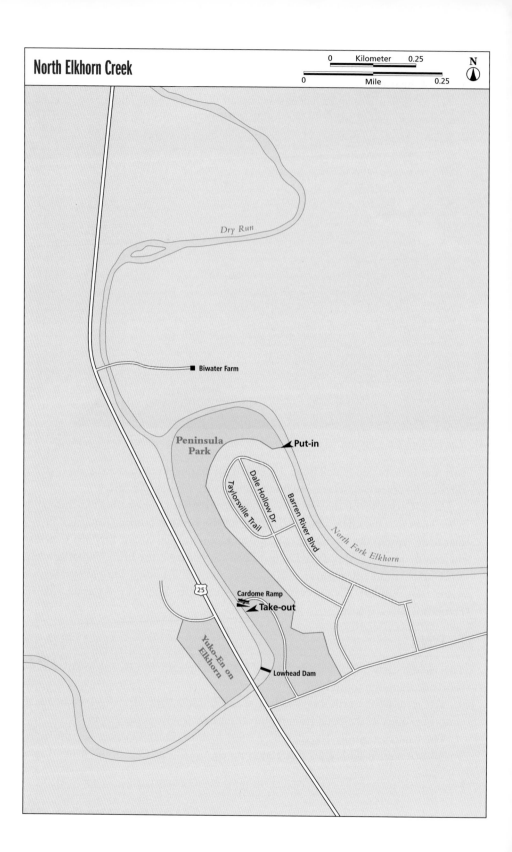

North Elkhorn Creek

sycamores, mixed with oaks, poplars, river birch, and willows, provide shade along the edges of the stream.

Dry Creek makes an excellent side trip off the main creek. The narrow waterway travels north and is sunken below the U.S. 25 roadway that parallels the roadway as it heads toward Bi-Water Farm. A thick strip of vegetation shields the view of the roadway and blocks much of the traffic noise. One can almost forget they are in the center of a busy suburban neighborhood.

A concrete bridge, decorated in the summer with bright hanging flowers, is 0.2 mile upstream. Smallmouth bass enjoy hanging along the rock shelf at the shoreline. It's possible to travel further upstream into Dry Creek, but the bridge is a nice place to turn around and head back into North Elkhorn Creek.

At the mouth of the creek, go right to continue downstream toward the take-out. Peninsula Park is located all along the inside of the bend. The take-out is on the left at mile 1.2. Don't miss it. The low head dam is just a tenth of a mile downstream. These dams are extremely dangerous and should not be run under any circumstances.

25 Floyd's Fork of the Salt River

Paddlers float through the heart of the Parklands of the Floyd as it winds its way southward, utilizing two of the new public paddling access points. (It is possible to bike between access points.) The float crosses through Beckley Creek Park before floating through an area of private but wooded property and ending just on the edge of Pope Lick Park upstream from the infamous Pope Lick Railroad Trestle. The 772-foot-long trestle, still utilized by the Norfolk Southern Railroad, is, according to urban legend, home to a mythical half-man, half-goat monster that lures victims onto the tracks where they are run down by a locomotive.

County: Jefferson

Start: North Beckley Paddling Access
N 38 13.1811 W 85 28.103

End: Fisherville Paddling Access
N 38 11.279', W 85 28.562'

Distance: 6.3 miles

Float Time: 3 hours, 30 minutes

Difficulty: Moderate, due to shoals and grass islands

Rapids: I

River Type: Suburban stream

Current: Slow to moderate

River Gradient: 4.5 feet per mile

River Gauge: USGS Floyds Fork at Pewee Valley, Fisherville. The best level to float the creek is between 90 cfs and 500 cfs. The best conditions to avoid dragging occur at 200 cfs. Between 500 and 1,000 cfs, paddling is for experienced boaters only. It is not recommended above 1,000 cfs, and at 2,000 cfs, access may be closed due to flood conditions.

The Parklands of the Floyds website shows current flow levels in the upper right corner of its homepage at www.theparklands.org.

Land Status: Public/private

Nearest City/Town: Middletown

Boats Used: Canoe, Kayak

Season: Winter, spring, fall, summer after rains

Fees or Permits: No

Maps: USGS Fisherville

Organizations: Parklands of the Floyd, www.theparklands.org, (502) 584-0350

Contacts/Outfitters: Blue Moon Canoe and Kayak of Kentucky, Floyd Community Building in Pope Lick Park, 4002 South Pope Lick Road, Louisville, KY 40299, (502) 753-9942, bluemooncanoeky.com

Getting There

To Shuttle Point/Take-out: From Middletown, take Shelbyville Road (U.S. 60) approximately 2 miles to the entrance ramp of I-265 West toward Louisville. In 4.5 miles, take exit 23 to Ky. 155/Taylorsville Road. Using the left lanes, turn left onto Ky. 155 in 1.5 miles, turn right onto Hatmaker Trail, and then make an almost immediate left onto Old Taylorsville Road. The parking lot for the Fisherville Access and take-out will be on the right.

To Put-in from Take-out: From the Fisherville Paddling Access parking lot, head east on Old Taylorsville Road for a half mile. Turn left onto South English Station Road, following it for 0.7 mile. Turn right onto Echo Trail, following it for 2.8 miles. Turn left

Former Kentucky Lt. Gov. Steve Henry and Kentucky Waterways Alliance Director David Wicks discuss Floyd's Fork conservation efforts during a paddle with author Carrie Stambaugh.
PROSPER MEDIA

onto Shelbyville Road, travel 0.6 miles, and then turn left onto Blue Heron Road. The parking lot for the North Buckley Paddle Access is on the right after 0.6 mile.

River Overview

Floyd's Fork is a 62-mile-long creek and tributary of the Salt River that begins in Henry County and flows 30 miles through Jefferson County before entering the Salt River in Bullitt County. Floyd's Fork is named for John Floyd, an early surveyor.

The creek is the namesake for the Parklands of Floyd's Fork, which consists of five Louisville public parks linked by a 27-mile stretch of Floyd's Fork. Floyd's Fork also benefits from the Future Fund Land Trust, which was established in 1993 to set aside 10,000 acres to protect its watershed. To date, 4,000 acres are preserved.

The Paddle

The paddle begins at the North Beckley paddling access in Beckley Creek Park. The river flows gently in this first stretch between the park's Louisville Loop and the Midland Golf Course. At the 0.5-mile point, the river takes a solid right-hand turn as it enters the stretch known as the Oxbow, a lazy stretch of slow-moving water that is stocked with rainbow trout and is also a favorite locale for spotted bass and sunfish. As the river turns back on itself, the next half mile is marked by a series of small islands. Stay in the main channel to avoid dragging bottom. At mile 1.6, you cross under the Beckley Creek Bridge with its signature leaping deer. Just before you cross under it, note the strong stream of water entering the river. This is the outflow of clean, cool water from the Metropolitan Sewer District.

PARKLANDS OF THE FLOYD

In 2005, the nonprofit 21st Century Parks was formed by a group of Louisville citizens to create a vision for the preservation and development of new parks in the Louisville Metro Area. The creation of the Parklands of Floyds Fork was launched with construction on park facilities beginning in 2011. As additional funds were raised—more than $120 million in all—additional projects were completed. In 2012, about 200 acres of Beckley Creek Park opened, with the remainder opening in 2013, along with Pope Lick Park.

Work on the final phase began that year and would include The Strand, Turkey Run, and Broad Run Parks. Turkey Run opened in October 2015 followed by Broad Run in April 2016 and finally The Strand in September 2016.

The project provided one hundred miles of new hiking and biking trails and a 19.7-mile canoe trail and six canoe launches, in addition to playgrounds, picnic areas, recreational fields, and dog parks.

Together the parks provide more than 4,000 acres of public recreation area, including 2,000 acres of forestland, 400 acres of restored meadow land, and 50 acres of restored wetlands. Approximately 7 miles of streambed were restored as part of the project, which aimed to preserve a 15-mile stretch of urban habitat.

At mile 1.4, you cross under the I-64 bridge. Four islands mark this stretch, and in general, they should be navigated on the right side. As you pass the park's famous Egg Lawn, the river bends to the right, and large water willows mark the banks, which are steep in this area. At mile 1.9, pass under a second leaping deer bridge; this is the Thorton Bridge. The Creekside Access, marked by a set of steps, is just beyond it on river right (west) at mile 2.

The river then makes a curve to the left and flows through some narrow channels and bars before entering the stretch called The Flats. This section can be very shallow but has fun waves and riffles when the water is higher. At mile 2.9 reach the third leaping deer bridge, known as the Sara and W. L. Lyons Bridge.

The next series of pools is marked by a steep cliff to the left, and as it makes a sharp turn to the right at mile 3, it passes through the remains of the Grosscurth Distillery Dam. The distillery burned to the ground in 1968, catching a portion of the river on fire as spirits flowed into the water and floated on top. Stay to the right here to navigate the channels.

The next bridge is at mile 3.7. After crossing beneath it, the river flows through private land until it reaches the Fisherville Take-out. Just past the 4-mile mark, Long Run enters the creek from the left (east).

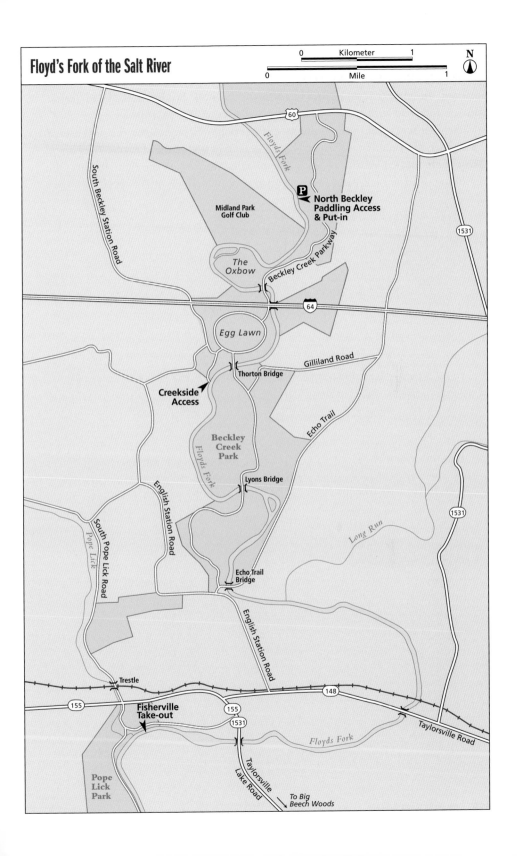

Floyd's Fork of the Salt River

The next stretch passes the Petersen Walnut Plantation—the largest east of the Mississippi—that is now being managed by Louisville Metro Parks for conservation purposes. At mile 5.1, you cross beneath the Norfolk Southern Railroad Trestle, which is followed at mile 5.2 by the Taylorsville Road (Ky. 148) Bridge.

The river flows past the community of Fisherville as it approaches the final bridge, the Taylorsville Lake Road Bridge (Ky. 155) at mile 6.2. The Fisherville Access and take-out are located less than a tenth of a mile downstream on the right. It marks the beginning of Pope Lick Park.

26 Kentucky River / Dix River

This is a paddle through one of the most historically significant stretches of the Kentucky River to the Dix River (tailwaters of Herrington Lake). The paddle is scenic with views of High Bridge, the Dixie Belle, and the Kentucky River Palisades.

Counties: Mercer, Jessamine, Garrad
Start and End: High Bridge Boat Ramp (Frankie's), 555 Lock 7 Road, Wilmore, KY 40390
N 37 49.555', W 84 43.416'
Distance: 8 miles
Float Time: 4 hours
Difficulty: Moderate, due to current and river traffic
Rapids: I
River Type: Wide, commercial water and dam-controlled tailwaters
Current: Slow to moderate
River Gradient: 1 foot per mile

River Gauge: USGS Kentucky River at Lock 10/Winchester. The minimum reading should be 800 cfs.
Land Status: Public/private
Nearest City/Town: Wilmore
Boats Used: Canoe, Kayak, SUP
Season: All
Fees or Permits: Launch fee of $4 per canoe or kayak
Maps: USGS Wilmore
Organizations: Jessamine County Trails Association www.jessaminetrails.com, (859) 885-2310 ext. 1014, jessaminecotrailsassociation@gmail.com
Contacts/Outfitters: High Bridge Boat Launch: (859) 368-3644

Getting There

To Put-in/Take-out: From Wilmore, head southwest on Ky. 29 for 4 miles, and then keep right to continue onto Pleasant Hill Road. In 0.3 mile, take a sharp right onto Lock 7 Road. In 0.4 mile, the entrance to Frankie's High Bridge Boat Ramp is on the left.

River Overview

The Kentucky River Palisades is a 100-mile section of river from Clay's Ferry in Madison County to Frankfort in Franklin County that passes through 450-million-year-old limestone cliffs that soar to 400 feet. Specifically, the cliffs are Lexington limestone—composed of thin limestone and interbedded shale. The forest along this stretch of river is the largest remaining in the inner Bluegrass region and supports the unique ecosystem of the area, which also consists of steep gorges and an intricate cave system fed by a spring. The forest itself is comprised of beech and yellow poplars, which grow on the terraces and banks of the river's tributaries. The steep slopes and higher elevations contain blue ash, chinquapin oak, sugar maple, rock elm, yellowwood, and yellow buckeye.

The Paddle

The paddle begins at the private boat ramp just upstream from Lock 7. Immediately upon entering the water, from the north bank, turn left to head upriver. I'd suggest crossing the river here to better inspect the 115-passenger paddle wheeler, The Dixie Bell, which is docked at Shaker Landing when it is not cruising. (Tours are offered daily from May to October.) There is a public landing at Shaker Village, which provides an alternative access and launch. Shaker Landing is on the south bank, 0.3 of a mile upriver from the launch.

Another 0.2 mile past the Dixie Belle, at 0.5 mile, you cross under High Bridge, which soars 275 feet above the river. High Bridge is an active railroad bridge connecting Jessamine and Mercer Counties. In use today by the Southern Norfolk Railway, it was first constructed in 1876 by the Cincinnati Southern Railway. It was the first cantilever bridge in the United States and is a National Civil Engineering Landmark. In 1911, the current structure, which contains three spans of upper deck trusses stretching 1,125 feet, was built around the existing structure, and in 1929, it

The Kentucky River passes beneath High Bridge near the historic Shaker Village where the paddle wheeler Dixie Belle now docks. CARRIE STAMBAUGH

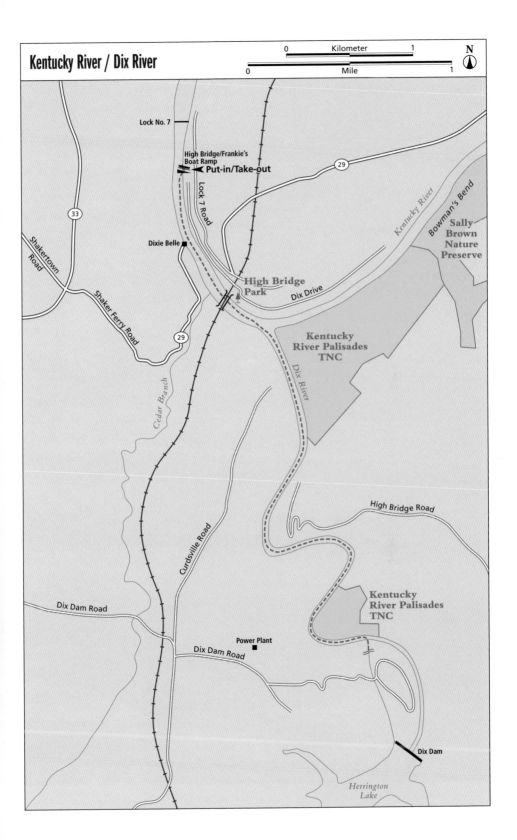

A small rapid on the Dix River along one of the most scenic stretches of the Kentucky's Palisades. CARRIE STAMBAUGH

was expanded to include two tracks. There's a good chance you'll see or hear a train using it during your paddle.

Upriver at mile 0.7 is the mouth of the Dix River, which enters the Kentucky River from the south. This section of the Dix River is downstream from the Herrington Lake Dam, and, therefore, is also known as the Tailwaters of Herrington Lake Dam. The water flow is swift and cold from the dam, and as a result, the stream is noted for its trout fishing in this section. In the summer, heavy mist often rises off the water, especially following a rainstorm, giving the paddle an almost surreal atmosphere at times.

Three miles of the Dix River flows between soaring cliffs and rocky outcroppings, which are heavily forested for the most part—although you may see some cows in one section, where a farm takes advantage of a valley—can be paddled easily.

The river gently curves as it passes through the high cliff walls, and at mile 3.7, there is a small waterfall in a tiny cove on the western bank. The water trickles down rock steps covered in moss. At mile 4.1, the upstream paddle is blocked by a rapid, squeezed between a rocky, overgrown peninsula of land and a high palisade wall. It is possible to portage around the rapid (a solid Class II) to reach the dam's overspill area.

I prefer to turn around here. The wave train coming from the rapid is a fun place to "play" and practice whitewater skills, including "peeling out" of the current as well as Eskimo Rolls.

27 Taylorsville Lake

This is a loop paddle that can be shortened or easily extended. This paddle is near the eastern headwaters of the lake where the main channel of the Salt River enters the reservoir. The eastern end of the lake is much shallower and narrower than other portions and, therefore, is less popular for use by motorized watercraft. It is surrounded by the Taylorsville Wildlife Management Area, which includes forested areas as well as a number of open, wildlife grazing areas.

Counties: Anderson, Spencer, Nelson
Start and End: Van Buren Boat Ramp (Taylorsville Lake State Park)
N 37 58.424', W 85 09.481'
Distance: 4.6 miles
Float Time: Approximately 2 hours
Difficulty: Easy
Rapids: None
River Type: Lake
Current: None
River Gradient: None
River Gauge: USGS 03295597. Lake level can be found at http://waterdata.usgs.gov/nwis or at www.lrl.usace.army.mil

Land Status: Public
Nearest City/Town: Anderson
Boats Used: Canoe, Kayak, SUP
Season: Any
Fees or Permits: No
Maps: USGS Chaplin
Organizations: US Army Corps of Engineers, Louisville District, (502) 477-8882
Kentucky Department of Fish and Wildlife, (502) 477-9024
Contacts/Outfitters: Taylorsville Lake State Park, 1320 Park Road, Mount Eden, KY 40046, (502) 477-0086, www.parks.ky.gov/parks/recreationparks/taylorsville-lake

Getting There

To Put-in/Take-out: This paddle uses the same put-in and take-out. Take U.S. 60 West from Lexington approximately 10 miles to the Bluegrass Parkway toward Lawrenceburg. Go east on the parkway for 12 miles to Ky. 127. Follow Ky. 127 North 4 miles, and then turn left on U.S. 62 West (Fox Creek Road). Follow for 15 miles, then turn right onto County Road 248, and follow it west for 4.1 miles before turning left on Van Buren Road/County Road 1579 South. Drive 1.7 miles. The roadway ends at the parking area and boat ramp inside the Taylorsville Lake WMA.

River Overview

Taylorsville Lake is a 3,050-acre man-made flood control lake on the Salt River. The dam is located approximately 60 river miles upriver from the Salt River's confluence with the Ohio River. The river was named for the various salt works that were located along its length in the 1800s. Construction on Taylorsville Lake was authorized under the Flood Control Act of 1966. Work began in 1974 on the reservoir, which drains an area of more than 350 square miles above the dam. It was completed

The shallow, narrow upper end of Taylorsville Lake provides serene paddling away from the busy main lake. CARRIE STAMBAUGH

by the US Army Corps of Engineers in 1983 and serves not only to prevent flooding but as a recreational site and a source of drinking water for nearby communities.

All 78 shoreline miles of the lake are public, and it is surrounded by more than 10,000 acres of mostly forested wildlife habitat managed by both the US Army Corps of Engineers and the Kentucky Department of Parks. The lake is known for having murky water year-round, which is mostly due to silt being washed in from upriver agricultural land. Standing timber is located throughout the lake and is an important source of protection for the lake's wildlife. The lake is known for its blue heron and is a popular destination for anglers boasting healthy populations of bass, crappie, catfish, and perch. Portions of the lake are also popular with boaters, which is why the paddle outlined in this book takes place on a quieter, more remote portion.

The Paddle

This is a loop paddle that begins at the Van Buren Boat Ramp at the end of County Road 1579. This paddle is near the eastern headwaters of the lake, where the Salt River enters the reservoir and where waters are much shallower and narrower than other portions of the lake. It also includes a no-wake zone. It is, therefore, less popular for use by motorized watercraft and provides a nice place for paddling.

The lake is approximately 0.25 mile wide at the put-in and is surrounded by forests and open meadows. Heading east (left from boat ramp) upstream toward the headwaters, the lake continues to narrow and become shallower. A number of islands, both permanent and seasonal, based on water levels, are in this area, so be mindful of standing timber and other obstructions below the surface. The paddling is easy, and the waters are usually calm with a gentle downstream current.

This area of the lake is prime for wildlife viewing, wading birds—most notably blue heron—and a number of other wildlife species, including deer and wild turkey, which are frequent visitors to its shoreline.

On the trip out, hug the rockier southern shoreline as it curves first south and then makes a U-turn north at mile 1.4. As you make the turn, the bridge of County Road 248 comes into view.

On the northern shore, there is a narrow entrance to a small lagoon area at mile 1.6, just before the lake crosses under the bridge at mile 1.8. The lagoon is a nice place to float and make a few casts. It is a popular place for shore anglers, so be mindful of their lines when entering this area.

Continue upriver under the bridge, and continue to hug the southern bank. At mile 2.1, a small tributary comes in on the southern side, and an island sits at the confluence. This is a particularly scenic area and a good place for a picnic before circling the island and heading back to the put-in.

I hugged the northern side of the river on my return trip, which includes a narrow strip of forested land, dominated by large trees including maples, oaks, and sycamores. Just beyond the trees is a cleared meadow, which boasts a spectacular display

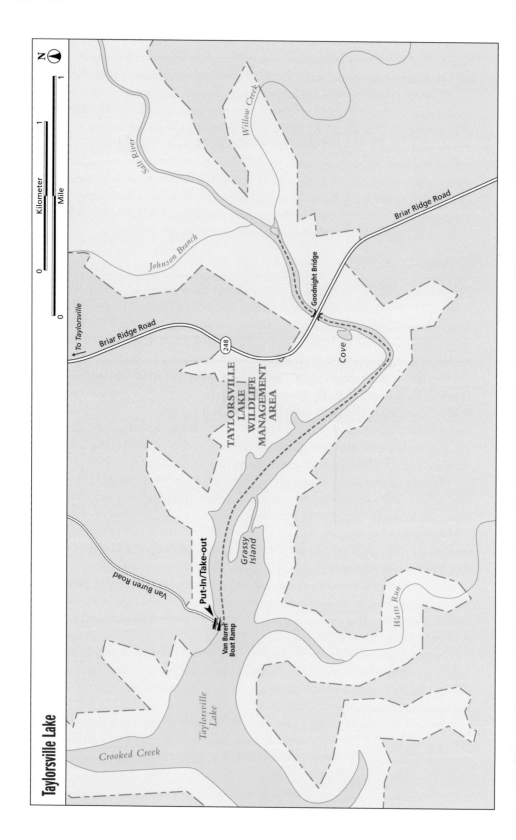

Taylorsville Lake

Taylorsville Lake's upper end is shallow and quiet, providing many scenic options for paddlers.
Carrie Stambaugh

of wildflowers in May. But beware, the bank can be extremely muddy in this area, making the short hike to the meadow a complicated one.

On the return trip, you will pass a number of other small, shallow coves on the northern bank, which appear first at mile 3.6 and then at mile 3.8. Both coves are popular places to see wading birds or simply areas to float out of the current of the main lake. The boat ramp and parking lot will come into view at mile 4, but they are another 0.6 mile away.

Western Kentucky

28 Ohio River / Beargrass Creek

This paddle is the definition of urban stream paddling. It explores a portion of the Ohio River along the Louisville riverfront and Beargrass Creek, a historical waterway that flows through the Butchertown neighborhood in the heart of Kentucky's biggest city.

County: Jefferson
Start and End: Louisville Rowing Club Boathouse Dock, 1501 Fulton Street, Louisville, Kentucky
N 38 15.836', W 85 43.883'
Distance: 3 miles
Float Time: 1 to 2 hours
Difficulty: Moderate, due to commercial traffic
Rapids: None
River Type: Wide, commercial, urban waterway and urban stream
Current: Moderate
River Gradient: 1 fpm

River Gauge: USGS 02394500 Ohio River at Louisville
Land Status: Public/private
Nearest City/Town: Louisville
Boats Used: Canoe, Kayak, SUP
Season: Any
Fees or Permits: No
Maps: USGS Jefferson
Organizations: Beargrass Creek Alliance, www.kwalliance.org/what-we-do/watershed-planning/current-projects/beargrass-creek-alliance

Getting There

To Put-in/Take-out: The Louisville Rowing Club Boathouse is located at 1501 Fulton Street. The dock is around the backside of the Boathouse. The Boathouse is located off River Road, 1 mile east of the central downtown business district.

River Overview

Beargrass Creek's three branches—the Middle, Muddy, and South Forks—come together just east of downtown Louisville, just before the waterway enters the Ohio River. Portions of the creek have been rerouted dating back to the 1850s as the city has grown around it. It has been plagued by pollution, namely the city's overflowing sewer system. Despite its bad reputation, the creek provides a natural refuge and is surrounded on both sides at its mouth by public parklands including the Thurston Park, Louisville Champions Park, and the Waterfront Botanical Gardens, which are currently being constructed in a years-long, multi-phase project.

The Paddle

The paddle begins in the Ohio River at the boat ramp directly across from Towhead Island just on the outskirts of Thurston Park.

The Ohio River at Louisville is a popular urban paddling destination for canoers, kayakers, rowers, and dragon boats. PROSPER MEDIA

Head upriver (right or east) toward the mouth of Beargrass Creek. Along the way, pass the River Park Place Marina below the new Waterside at RiverPark Place apartments. At the end of Towhead Island, at mile 0.4, one can look north across the width of the river—a mile—to the Indiana shore, which is dominated by heavy industry.

Continue upstream to mile 0.6 to reach the mouth of Beargrass Creek. Turning right, head south down Beargrass Creek. The waterway instantly narrows and becomes shaded. Both sides of the creek are public parkland, with the western bank being the Waterfront Botanical Gardens and the east being the Louisville Champions Park. At mile 0.8, cross under the Butchertown Greenway Bridge, it is followed by the River Road Bridge and then a railroad bridge, all in quick succession. At mile 1, you cross under the twin I-71 bridges. This marks the end of public lands. The river

BEARGRASS CREEK ALLIANCE

Beargrass Creek is the object of a nonprofit organization Beargrass Creek Alliance. It was the subject of a 30-minute documentary, *Beargrass: The Creek in Our Backyard*, which was directed by award-winning film creator Morgan Atkinson and released in 2017.

Apocalypse Brew Works, located along the creek, used filtered creek water to create a beer, called Beargrass Creek Blonde, in its honor. Proceeds from the sale of the beer were donated to the Beargrass Creek Alliance's work to restore the watershed.

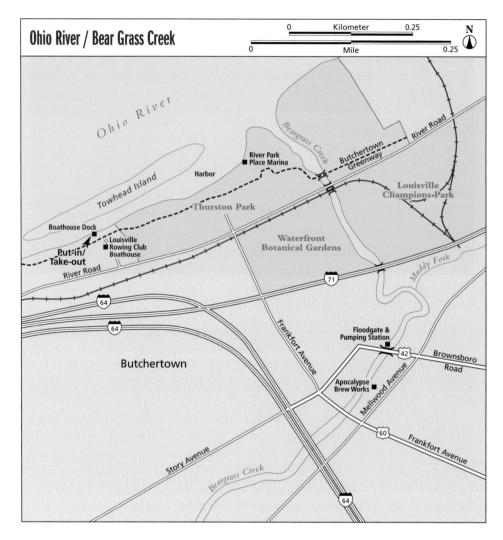

then makes a sharp turn to the left and then to the right. The Muddy Fork of Beargrass enters from the east. Notice the now-defunct gate of an old Combined Sewer Overflow to the right; above the river is the Police Impound lot.

At mile 1.3, pass through the towering floodgate, which controls the flow of Beargrass Creek into the Ohio River. At times of high water, this gate is shut to prevent the river from backing up into the highly populated Butchertown neighborhood of Louisville.

In less than a tenth of a mile, cross beneath Brownsboro Road. The next 0.2 mile stretch before the U.S. 60 Bridge is heavily wooded, shielding the river from the surrounding neighborhood. This is a good place to turn around and head back to the Boathouse.

29 Rolling Fork of the Salt River

This paddle along the Rolling Fork takes you through historic Kentucky countryside. Although born at Sinking Spring near Hodgenville, Kentucky, Abraham Lincoln grew up along Knob Creek in LaRue County. Knob Creek is a tributary of the Rolling Fork that flows into the river near the end of this paddle. Knob Creek begins just east of Hodgenville and ends just north of the town of New Haven in Nelson County. The Rolling Fork passes through rural countryside where a thick ribbon of trees up a steep muddy bank often separates the river from the surrounding farms.

Counties: LaRue, Nelson
Start: Below Ky. 31 bridge at Nelson / LaRue County line
N 37 34.383', W 85 36.318'
End: Just past Ky. 52 bridge south of New Haven at the Nelson / LaRue line. Behind the New Haven First and Last Chance Bar and Liquor Store.
N 37 39.062', W 85 35.851'
Distance: 15.1 miles
Float Time: 4 hours
Difficulty: Moderate, due to shoals and distance
Rapids: I, II

River Type: Pastoral stream with rocks and shoals
Current: Slow to moderate
River Gradient: 2.1 feet per mile
River Gauge: USGS 03301500 Rolling Fork River near Boston, KY. Minimum reading should be 400 cfs.
Land Status: Private
Nearest City/Town: New Haven
Boats Used: Canoe, Kayak, SUP
Season: Spring, summer, fall
Fees or Permits: No fees or permits required
Maps: USGS New Haven, Howardstown

Getting There

To Shuttle Point/Take-out: The take-out is in New Haven off Ky. 52 next to the New Haven First and Last Chance Bar and Liquor Store at 101 South Main Street.
To Put-in from Take-out: Turn from Ky. 52 onto U.S. 31 East. Follow it for 5.9 miles before turning left onto Ky. 84 east toward Lebanon. After 3.7 miles, cross a highway bridge over the river and turn right on a gravel road that leads to parking and the put-in. The bridge is located on the border of LaRue and Nelson Counties, and the put-in is below it.

River Overview

The Rolling Fork begins in Boyle County and flows through Marion County before forming the border between LaRue and Nelson County and making a large U as it winds through the region known as the Knobs. The river lies in valleys between the knobs—isolated, cone-shaped hills—and farm fields. It is mostly hidden from the world around it by a thick belt of trees as it flows through this still largely rural area.

The Rolling Fork of the Salt River flows through the historic Knobs area, passing near President Abraham Lincoln's boyhood home at Knob Creek. CARRIE STAMBAUGH

The river has several notable tributaries, including Knob Creek and Pottinger Creek, which both flow into the river along this paddle. Colonel Samuel Pottinger, a member of James Harrod's company, set up a pioneer station here in 1781. Knob Creek, where Abraham Lincoln lived for about 5 years of his childhood, is also a notable tributary.

The Rolling Fork originates in Boyle County in Central Kentucky, flowing 108 miles before emptying into the Salt River about 9 miles upstream from its confluence with the Ohio River.

The Paddle

This paddle is refreshingly remote and has a wilderness feel to it, as the river is hidden below a heavy tree line for most of the paddle. The Knobs rise above the river on either side, and on my paddle, I spotted an abundance of wildlife along this route.

The river does rise and fall rapidly following heavy rains, so be sure to check local water gauges and beware that the banks can be extremely slick and muddy, as was the case on this paddle. The gauge at Boston in Nelson County read 2,000 cfs and measured the water level at 12 feet and falling the day of this paddle.

After launching and floating below the Ky. 84 Bridge, the river winds between steep, muddy banks for the first 2 miles. It is approximately 35 to 40 feet wide, and tulip poplars, sycamores, and a variety of maples and oaks line the riverbanks here, and there are many downed trees along the edges of the river.

After making a sharp bend at mile 2.5, a road comes into view high above the river, reminding paddlers of the civilization around them. At mile 3.1, power lines cross the river, and the first home comes into view on river left. At mile 3.9, a tire swing hangs from a tree near a nice gravel beach on river left. It was here that I spotted an otter trolling along the banks.

The river continues its winding path between steep, wooded banks, and at mile 5.9, it passes beneath another electric line. The river has widened by this point to about 55 feet and continues to be hidden by thick trees and high knobs on both sides with banks about 10 feet high and muddy. Although I experienced no downed trees that could not be easily navigated around, low water levels could make this section tricky. There are many trees leaning heavily across the water as well as exposed roots on this stretch.

At mile 6.2, I spotted a large stand of river cane, a native species of bamboo. Now an endangered ecosystem, cane breaks were once common along Kentucky waterways. The river makes a large curve here to river right and opens up to meadows and farm fields on either side. The water is relatively flat in this area, and as it passes under power lines at mile 7.2, rock banks begin to take over. At mile 7.3, fallen rocks on the right create a small rapid with a fun little wave train as the river curves toward river left.

This stretch is particularly scenic. Small waterfalls from tributaries are common here, and the thin, exposed shale layers below the limestone caprock of the banks are exposed on either side. At mile 8.9, Blanton Road appears above the river on river right. It was here that I spotted a beaver, scurrying down the muddy bank and into the water as we passed. At mile 9, just before the river flows beneath a small bridge, a put-in appears on river left. Above the river is a large white house. This would be a good alternative take-out or put-in.

At mile 10, the largest tributary of the float flows into the river from the east. This is Pottinger Creek. At mile 10.7, in a large curve, there is a high grassy bank and a private put-in. This would make an excellent lunch spot in dry weather, as over the next tenth of a mile, the banks rise again and steep hillsides come straight down to the river. This is the area known as the Devil's Backbone and where a local folktale says two young lovers leaped to their death.

By mile 12, the steep hills are gone, and the river flattens out some and is lined by flat farm fields, we paddled alongside a farmer on his tractor during this stretch.

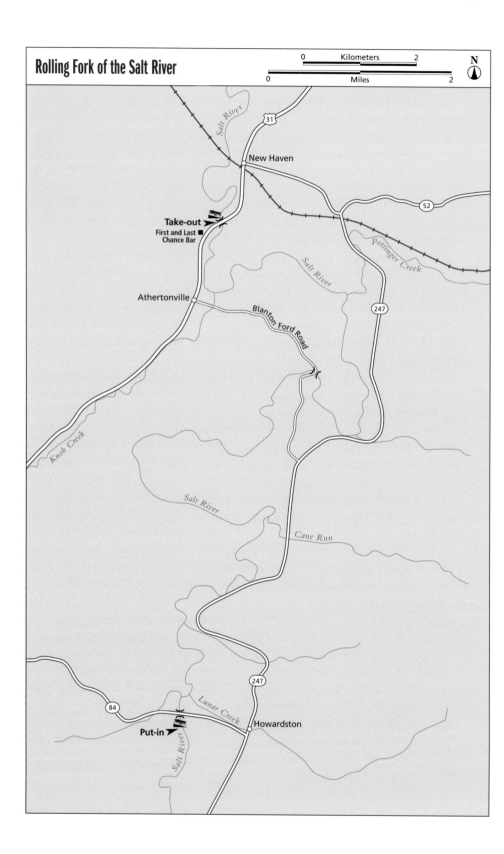

Rolling Fork of the Salt River

Kilometers 0 2

Miles 0 2

N

New Haven

31

52

Take-out
First and Last
Chance Bar

Salt River

Pottinger Creek

Athertonville

Blanton Ford Road

247

Salt River

Knob Creek

Salt River

Cane Run

247

84

Lunar Creek

Put-in

Howardston

Salt River

The water was calm and the river wider in this stretch, perhaps reaching a width of about 70 feet.

At mile 13.9, the river makes a lazy turn, and high rock banks line the river, but flat farm fields can be seen above it. At mile 14.3, a local roadway comes into view on river right, and a large stretch of rip-rap bank. Power lines cross the river here, and on river left, there is a small put-in as well. At mile 15.1, cross under the U.S. 31 East Bridge and immediately begin looking for the take-out on river right. The take-out here is steep and muddy, so use caution.

30 Lost River Cave

This is one of the only places in Kentucky where paddlers can view the state's underground geology by boat.

County: Warren
Start and End: Lost River Cave Entrance
N 36 57.215', W 86 28.380'
Distance: 1 mile
Float Time: 45 minutes
Rapids: None
River Type: Underground
Current: Moderate
River Gradient: n/a
River Gauge: n/a
Land Status: Private
Nearest City/Town: Bowling Green
Boats Used: Guided tours on metal boats or kayaks are available. No private boats allowed.

Season: Boat tours are available from March to September. Kayak trips are offered March to May only.
Fees or Permits: Yes. Private kayaking cave tours are $36 per person. These guided trips are offered via reservations only between March and May. The tours are open to adults and children ages six and up.
Maps: USGS Bowling Green South
Organizations: Western Kentucky University, Friends of Lost River Cave
Contacts/Outfitters: Friends of Lost River Cave, (270) 393-0077, http://www.lostriver cave.org

River Overview

The Lost River originates above ground, flowing in three short sections before descending into a 7-mile cave system. The river is accessible via one of the largest natural underground entrances in the eastern United States.

This paddle truly is a one-of-a-kind Kentucky experience. All tours begin at the mouth of the cave, which is the lowest elevation in a roughly 55-square-mile area. Approximately 150 feet across and about 45 feet high from riverbed to ceiling, the entrance is located below 45 feet of limestone bedrock. The cave has been a well-known and well-used local feature for the last 10,000 years. Its first appearance in recorded history is 1792.

Lost River Cave preserves an interesting set of geological features. The trip through it is really a small hike and a paddle. After leaving the visitor center, visitors walk a short distance through the woods and descend along a dirt path through the forest to the valley floor and the headwaters of the Lost River.

The first stop is Blue Hole, which is a pool of bright, mysterious, bluish-green water. The tint comes from calcite in the limestone bedrock of Kentucky, which gets washed out whenever it rains. When this is mixed with carbon dioxide, it makes carbonic acid. Calcite is white and, therefore, easily reflects the blue of the sky and the green of the leaf cover above it.

Lost River Cave is open to boat tours, includling kayak tours on selected dates.
CARRIE STAMBAUGH

Lost River's Blue Hole and cave entrance are located in a bowl. In times of heavy rains, it gets inundated with runoff and, most recently in 2010, recorded water depths of more than 66 feet at the cave entrance!

The feature was legendary in folklore for swallowing unlucky people and animals. According to guides, the hole is mentioned for the first time in local history in 1861. During the Civil War, Confederate troops from Tennessee claimed Bowling Green as the Confederate state capitol.

Soldiers used the large mouth of Lost River Cave to store ammunition. To ferry in and out supplies, they built a steep dirt trail down to the cave entrance. A mule team and wagoner once reportedly careened off the path into the Blue Hole and were never seen again.

Later, after Union troops overran the area, four young soldiers were taking a dip in the cool waters. One of them decided he'd dive to the bottom, pick up a rock, and bring it to the surface to prove the Confederates had been lying to them about the bottomless blue hole.

See the stalactites and stalagmites by flashlight on a guided paddle or boat tours of Lost River Cave. CARRIE STAMBAUGH

When he failed to surface, a second soldier descended. He too didn't surface, and a third soldier then dove to rescue his friends. After a few minutes, the fourth climbed from the pool and ran for help. He added to the lore of the hole by proclaiming it a man-eater, too.

Next, the railroad company began using the "bottomless" pit to fill its steam engines. A team of engineers tried to measure it, using a rock and rope. The deepest point they found was 437 feet deep.

In 1985, after the land was donated to Western Kentucky University, Professor Nicholas Crawford, the director of the school's Center for Caves and Karst studies, measured the depth of the pool at 16 feet. He then determined the pool is a "karst window" leading to an underground river. Karst simply means an area of landscape underlain with caves created by water flowing through soluble limestone rocks.

The pool actually has several karst windows about 4 to 5 feet below the water surface, which allows water to flow in and out of the underground river, often creating a strong underwater current. More water flows out of the windows, however, than flows in, which creates an aboveground spillway that flows approximately 440 feet to the cave's entrance.

Various milling operations followed until the 1930s when its then-owner, Jimmy Stewart, began inviting visitors to the Cavern Nite Club in 1933 or 1934 following the repeal of Prohibition. The outflow of cool air, at a steady 57 degrees, created natural air-conditioning in a time before there was easy climate control.

Combined with its proximity to the Dixie Highway, the most highly traveled local roadway during the time, the club became a popular destination. The music of the day was jazz, big band, and swing music, and some of the most famous musicians of the time, including Ella Fitzgerald, Dinah Shore, Francis Craig, and the NBC Orchestra, are said to have performed here. In the 1940s, Mr. Stewart created a beer garden on the ridgeline overlooking the cave entrance and carved 150 stone stairs out of the cliff side leading down to the dance floor at the mouth of the cave.

By 1955, however, air-conditioning had been invented, the interstate system was introduced, and popular music changed to rock and roll. By 1965, the business was shuttered.

Unfortunately, over the next few decades, the cave became a local dumping ground. In 1986, the cave and twenty-five surrounding acres were donated to nearby Western Kentucky University.

A group of concerned local citizens eventually founded the Friends of Lost River in late 1990 and began removing debris. They also built a small dam in the back of the cave to create the pool of water that allows boat tours in the cave.

By 1998, 55 tons of trash were hauled out from the cave entrance, including large machinery such as farming equipment, appliances, a car, and a mobile home. The nonprofit operates from the funds visitors generate.

The Paddle

The cave entrance is 150 feet across about 45 feet high from riverbed to the ceiling of the cave. Above the cave ceiling is another 45 feet of limestone bedrock. This is where all watercraft are boarded for guided kayak and boat tours.

The trip inside the cave, lit by overhead lights, is mesmerizing.

Boaters paddle into several distinct "rooms" within the cave, viewing formations including flowstones. Other features have names like Bonsai Trees, Hot Air Balloons, and Sheep's Retreat.

Throughout the paddle, droplets of water, known as "cave kisses," drip from the ceiling. Small stalactites are visible on the ceiling, but the largest is about 2-feet long and called "praying hands." Because the cave floods often, formations are often damaged by debris.

31 Drakes Creek

An easily accessible, peaceful paddle through a lushly wooded stream in the heart of one of Kentucky's fastest growing cities. Search for fossils in the gravel beds, and look out for waterfalls and gorgeous rock shelves. There is excellent fishing along the creek for a variety of fish including smallmouth, largemouth, and rock bass, as well as bluegill and muskellunge.

County: Warren
Start: Romanza Johnson County Park, Mount Lebanon Church Road
N 36 52.387', W 86 22.342'
End: Phil Moore Park, 7101 Scottsville Road, Alvaton, KY 42122 U.S. 231
N 36 53.719', W 86 22.853'
Distance: 6 miles
Float Time: 2.5 to 4 hours
Difficulty: Easy to moderate, depending on current and river level
Rapids: I
River Type: Wooded, suburban stream
Current: Slow to swift
River Gradient: 2.4 feet

River Gauge: USGS West Fork Drakes Creek near Franklin. Minimum reading should be 150 cfs.
Land Status: Public/private
Nearest City/Town: Bowling Green
Boats Used: Canoe, Kayak, SUP
Season: Spring, summer, fall
Fees or Permits: No fees or permits required
Maps: USGS Drake, Allen Springs, Polkville, Bowling Green South
Organizations: Warren County Blueways, trailsrus.com/blueways
Contacts/Outfitters: Drakes Creek Canoe, LLC, DrakesCreekCanoe.com, (270) 781-3938

Getting There

To Shuttle Point/Take-out: From I-65 near Bowling Green, take William H. Natcher Green River Highway/Ky. 9007 North exit toward Bowling Green/Owensboro. Keep left at the fork, and continue to follow the signs for exit 20 A William H. Natcher Parkway. In 2.4 miles, merge onto U.S. 231 (Scottsville Road). In 0.7 mile, exit at Phil Moore Park on the right.

To Put-in from Take-out: Take U.S. 231 South for 2.3 miles. Turn right onto Mount Lebanon Church Road. In 0.8 mile, turn right onto Romanza Johnson Road. It is a half mile further to the boat ramp just before the road crosses over the Trammel Fork Creek.

River Overview

Drakes Creek is a tributary of the Barren River. It flows north from its start in Simpson and Allen Counties near the Tennessee border, through rolling forests and farmland toward Bowling Green. It provides excellent paddling and fishing opportunities. Its ease of access makes it a great float for families and a variety of watercraft.

Indian beads, fossilized stem segments of ancient marine animals, can be found along the banks of Drakes Creek. CARRIE STAMBAUGH

The Paddle

This float starts on the Trammel Fork of Drakes Creek just 0.3 mile before its confluence with Drakes Creek. The Trammel Fork is about 20 feet wide and heavily shaded,
with sloping, muddy banks rising 5 to 10 feet above the river.

The water, on my paddle, was obviously lower than it had been in the recent days,
and the banks were slick with mud. At the confluence, the creek suddenly widens to
twice its size but remains nestled between heavily wooded hillsides. It gently snakes
along, and at the 1.5-mile mark, in the elbow of the turn, there is a significant pile of
debris and logs, evidence of the creek's recent high level.

As the curve ends, the river straightens out for a stretch and reveals a view of large
trees leaning majestically out over the water, a stretch of gently swaying grass beds,
and a sloping gravel bar. A mother duck with a brood of fluffy ducklings floated by us
on this stretch, and a heron lazily glided further downstream in front of us here, too.

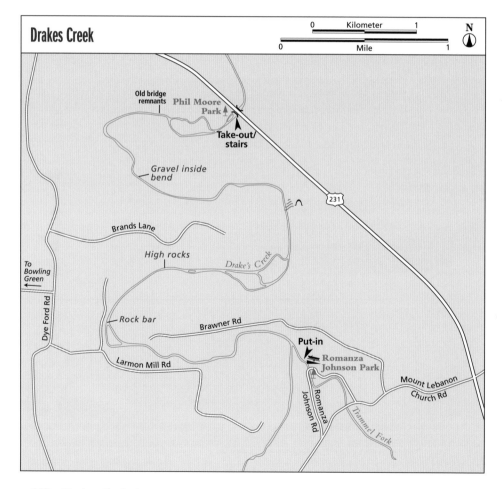

We also heard the distinctive "plop" of cautious turtles abandoning their sunny spots for the cool waters of the creek.

At mile 2.0, the river curves and high rocks appear on river left, giving it a distinct gorge-like feel. Stay right at the first gravel island to avoid having to drag. At mile 2.7, the river makes its next curve, and the high wall gives way to a muddy bank above, on which rests farm fields.

At mile 3.5, on river right is a lovely private riverside estate with a deck and lookout point; just past it, you may feel cool air forcing its way out of a small cave in the rocky hillside. Listen closely for falling water here.

At mile 4.5, a set of rippling gravel shoals makes for a bit of fun paddling before the river settles back down, flowing between soaring sycamores, oaks, and maples. There are several large gravel bars in this area, one of which we choose to stop upon for a picnic lunch.

Upon inspection of the gravel at our feet, we discovered abundant cylindrical fossils. We spent a few minutes collecting a pocketful of specimens. Later, we learned these fossils are called Indian beads and are the remnants of ancient sea creatures.

At mile 5.5, you pass the remnants of an old bridge, whose stone pylons it appears were cut directly from the rocky banks nearby. As you pass beneath the metal bridge, hug the bank at river right and notice the stadium lights of Philmore Park peaking high above the trees here.

As the river finishes a curve and prepares to enter another, a second bridge comes into view and so do the distinct disc golf nets along the manicured bank. The take-out is to the left at a concrete boat ramp just before the Ky. 231 Bridge. A set of stairs climbs up the riverbank. There is a second take-out exactly another mile downstream in the park.

32 Nolin River Lake

This is a lazy loop paddle, launching from and returning to the Wax Recreation Area Campground. It can be easily extended to a much longer paddle. The banks of the lake are protected by the Nolin River Lake Kentucky Wildlife Management Area, but beyond the shoreline is private property in much of the area of this paddle. The exception is the area of the campground, which is public property.

Counties: Hart, Grayson, Edmondson
Start and End: Wax Creek Campground
N 37 20.389', W 86 07.781'
Distance: 2.7 miles
Float Time: 2 to 3 hours
Difficulty: Easy
Rapids: None
River Type: Lake
Current: None
River Gradient: None
River Gauge: http://www.lrl-wc.usace.army
.mil/reports/lkreport.html
Land Status: Public/private
Nearest City/Town: Wax
Boats Used: Canoe, Kayak, SUP

Season: Spring, summer, fall
Fees or Permits: There is a $5 fee to park and launch a boat at USACE boat ramps. This fee is waived if you are overnight camping. An annual pass can be purchased for $40.
Maps: USGS Nolin Lake
Organizations: Kentucky Fish and Wildlife, Friends of Nolin River Lake, PO Box 11, Brownsville, KY 42210, (270) 286-8003, friendsof nolinlake.com, info@friendsofnolinlake.org
Contacts/Outfitters: US Army Corps of Engineers, Nolin River Lake USACE, 2150 Nolin Dam Road, PO Box 339, Bee Spring, KY 42207,
Wax Campground, (270) 242-7578

Getting There

To Put-in/Take-out: To the put-in, from Louisville, take I-65 South to exit 76, and then turn west onto Ky. 224. After 9 miles, turn left on Ky. 479, then continue for another 8 miles, and turn left onto Ky. 88. Continue into the campground entrance.

River Overview

The Nolin River begins in Hardin County and flows south, creating the Grayson–Hart County Line. The river flows through hilly farm country, bordered exclusively by private land until it reached Nolin River Lake. The banks are often steep, muddy, and rocky.

Nolin River Lake was created when the US Army Corps of Engineers impounded the Nolin River in 1963, acting under the Flood Control Act of 1938. The reservoir swells and shrinks in size from 2,890 acres at winter pool to 5,795 acres at summer pool.

Below the Nolin River Lake Dam, the river flows 7 miles to its confluence with the Green River within Mammoth Cave National Park. The river is extremely scenic

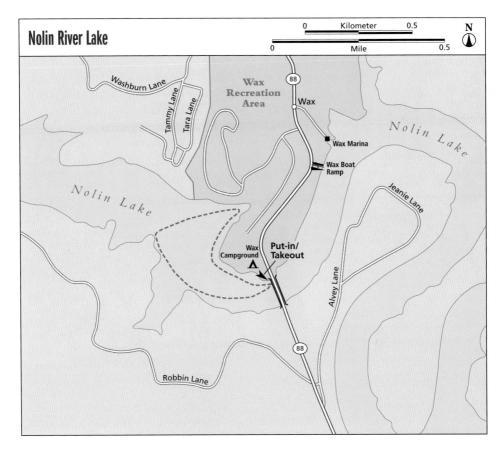

0   Kilometer   0.5

0   Mile   0.5

N

in this stretch, but unfortunately, it is no longer easy to paddle because of the removal of Lock and Dam No. 6 on the Green River in 2017 downstream from the confluence. The result is lower water levels that caused many trees to fall across the narrow stream, making it nearly impossible to navigate at this time.

The Paddle

This paddle begins and ends at the Wax Recreation Area campground, which is an excellent place for a camping and canoe run.

The gently sloping shoreline from the campground is shaded by large trees, including sycamore, sweetgum, box elder, black walnut, sugarberry trees, and bald cypress, with their knobby knees sticking out of the water along the shoreline. Thickets of buttonbush were blooming along the shoreline during our visit in early July, attracting hordes of butterflies and bees. The fishing is excellent for a variety of species and can be done from a boat or the shore.

Launching from the campground, head east to cross under the Ky. 88 Bridge. Hug the northern shoreline, turning to the north at the opening of a large cove. This area

The shore of Nolin River Lake is shaded with large cypress trees and other hardwoods at the campground near Wax, Kentucky. CARRIE STAMBAUGH

is somewhat protected from the busy main lake traffic, making it a great place for hand-powered craft to explore.

The lake is about a half mile wide in this area, and as you head east, it narrows still further. Heading west, the lake widens, and motorized boat traffic increases in the main channel of the lake. During the summer traffic can be quite heavy, but there are often canoes and kayaks on the water, launching from the campground during the summer months, as well as swimmers along the shorelines.

33 Green River Lake

This is a loop paddle on Green River Lake that starts and ends at the Holmes Creek Marina boat ramp. It can easily be shortened or expanded. The lake makes a horseshoe turn here, widening and then narrowing. High rock walls dominate the southern bank of the river, which is heavily forested, although the occasional house or structure peaks out from among the trees. The northern bank of the river is more accessible, although it can vary too from almost vertical rock to sloping gravel banks. The area is a popular waterfowl hunting location, and blinds dot the shoreline.

County: Adair
Start and End: Holmes Bend Marina
N 37 13.294', W 85 16.099'
Distance: 4.6 miles
Float Time: 3 hours
Difficulty: Easy
Rapids: None
River Type: Lake
Current: None
River Gradient: None
River Gauge: http://www.lrl-wc.usace.army
.mil/reports/lkreport.html
Land Status: Public/private
Nearest City/Town: Columbia
Boats Used: Canoe, Kayak, SUP
Season: Spring, summer, fall

Fees or Permits: There is a $5 fee to park and launch a boat at USACE boat ramps. This fee is waived if you are overnight camping. An annual pass can be purchased for $40.
Maps: USGS Cane Valley, Green River Lake Army Corps of Engineers Map
   Organizations: Green River Lake State Park, 179 Park Office Road, Campbellsville, KY 42718, (270) 465-8255, www.parks.ky.gov
   USACE Holmes Bend, 69 Corps Road, Columbia, KY, 42728, (270) 384-4623
   Corps of Engineers Office, (270) 465-4463
Contacts/Outfitters: Green River Canoeing Inc, 209 Campbellsville, KY (270) 789-2956, mammothcavecanoe.com, GreenRiverLake.com

Getting There

To Put-in/Take-out: From Columbia, take Cumberland Parkway to exit 49 and merge onto Ky. 55 North. Continue for 1.5 miles, and then turn right on Ky. 551. After a mile, turn left on Holmes Bend Road, following signs to the marina.

River Overview

The Green River, which flows 370 miles through the state, is one of Kentucky's most famous waterways. It is the longest river to flow exclusively through Kentucky, and it begins in Lincoln County and flows west to its confluence with the Ohio River across from Evansville, Indiana. The river drains twelve Kentucky counties, flows through Mammoth Cave National Park, and is impounded in Green River Lake.

Green River Lake was created in 1969 by the US Army Corps of Engineers as a flood control lake. The 8,210-acre lake has a surface area of 12.8 square miles and

A gravel and rock shore along Green River Lake is an excellent place to beach a paddlecraft for a swim. CARRIE STAMBAUGH

can hold in excess of 723,000 acre-feet of water. It is the largest lake in the USACE's Louisville District. Green River Lake has an average depth of 50 feet and can reach up to a mile in width at its largest point.

The Paddle

The paddle begins and ends at the Holmes Bend Marina and is a loop paddle in Corbin's Bend that can easily be enlarged in either direction. Begin by heading west from the boat launch, hugging the southern bank (the outside of Corbin's Bend) as it curves around a small peninsula of land jutting in from the north.

In 0.6 mile, there is a small cove that makes for an excellent place to float and cast a line.

Continuing out of the cove, which is approximately 0.2 mile across, cross the lake to reach the northern bank or the inside of the bend. The lake is 0.4 to 0.5 mile wide in this area. At this point, you are 1.2 miles into the paddle. Continue heading west, hugging the northern bank, where the shoreline slopes gently into the water. There are small stretches of gravel beach, but in most areas, trees and brush reach down to the water.

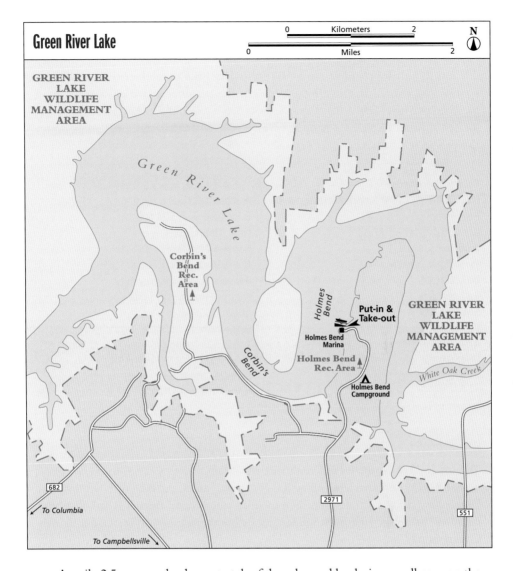

0   Kilometers   2

0   Miles   2

N

GREEN RIVER
LAKE
WILDLIFE
MANAGEMENT
AREA

Green River Lake

Corbin's
Bend
Rec.
Area

Holmes Bend

Put-in &
Take-out

GREEN RIVER
LAKE
WILDLIFE
MANAGEMENT
AREA

Holmes Bend
Marina

Holmes Bend
Rec. Area

Corbin's
Bend

White Oak Creek

Holmes Bend
Campground

682

2971

551

To Columbia

To Campbellsville

At mile 2.5, you reach a large stretch of sloped gravel banks in a small cove on the peninsula. This beach makes a nice place for swimming, and the gravel is abundant with fossils and interesting rocks.

This is a good place to turn around and head back to the put-in. There does seem to be a current along the southern bank in this section, so I would again recommend hugging the northern shore for easier paddling. It also is safely out of the way of motorboats. Arrive back at the marina for an approximately 4.6-mile paddle.

34 Rough River Lake

This quick little loop paddle on the Rough River Lake in the Laurel Brach Recreation area is located in roughly the center of the lake where two of its arms come together near the dam. A large island, protected as a Wildlife Management Area, is located adjacent to the boat ramp. A cove on its southern shore is the destination on this paddle, which can be easily extended to as long a paddle as desired.

County: Breckinridge
Start and End: Laurel Branch Recreation Area Boat Ramp
N 37 36.397', W 86 27.540'
Distance: 2 miles
Float Time: 2 hours
Difficulty: Easy
Rapids: None
River Type: Lake
Current: None
River Gradient: None
River Gauge: http://www.lrl-wc.usace.army .mil/reports/lkreport.html

Lake levels fluctuate. Levels are 470 feet at winter pool and summer pool at 495 feet. Flood state is at 524 feet.
Land Status: Public
Nearest City/Town: Leitchfield
Boats Used: Canoe, Kayak, SUP
Season: Spring, summer, fall
Fees or Permits: $5 day use fee
Maps: USGS McDaniels
Organizations: US Army Corps of Engineers, 14957 Falls of Rough Road, Falls of Rough, KY 40119-6318, (270) 257-2061
Contacts/Outfitters: Laurel Branch Campground, (270) 257-8839

Getting There

To Put-in/Take-out: From Leitchfield, take Main Street (Ky. 259) to the intersection of Ky. 737 and turn left. Follow Ky. 737 for 9.5 miles, and then turn left onto Ky. 259. Follow it for 3.5 miles, and then turn left onto Laurel Branch Road. The boat ramp will be on the right in 1.3 miles, just before the entrance to the Laurel Branch Campground.

River Overview

Rough River Lake is a 5,100-acre flood control lake, which was created in 1959 by the US Army Corps of Engineers.

The lake is located in Breckinridge, Grayson, and Hardin Counties in the "Clifty" area of Kentucky's Pennyroyal Area, marked by its layers of soluble limestone, which have resulted in sinks and caverns throughout the region.

The Rough River is a 156-mile tributary of the Green River, which originates in Hardin County. It flows west, southwest to its confluence with the Green near Livermore. The Rough River Dam is located upriver from Rough River Falls.

Rough River Lake is a popular summer swimming and boating destination. On weekends it can be crowded with paddled and motorized watercraft but is quiet on weekdays. CARRIE STAMBAUGH

The Paddle

This paddle begins and ends at the Laurel Branch Boat Ramp. In the summer, this lake is a very popular summer destination for pleasure boaters. The shore of the lake is a public Wildlife Management Area, but there are many private homes overlooking the lake.

Although motorized crafts are the most popular boats on the waterway, there has been a proliferation of smaller, human-powered craft in recent years. It is not uncommon to see large groups of paddlers on the lake, even during the middle of the day in the summer rush.

This paddle is best enjoyed, however, early or late on a weekday during the busy summer season or any day during the slower fall and spring months.

From the ramp, bear left, heading south along the shoreline for approximately a half mile to the cove where Laurel Branch enters this part of the lake. Being sure to look both ways across the channel, paddle 0.3 mile across the lake to arrive on the westernmost shore of the island at mile 0.8.

Paddle 0.2 mile further south into a narrow cove at mile 1. This is the turnaround spot for this paddle.

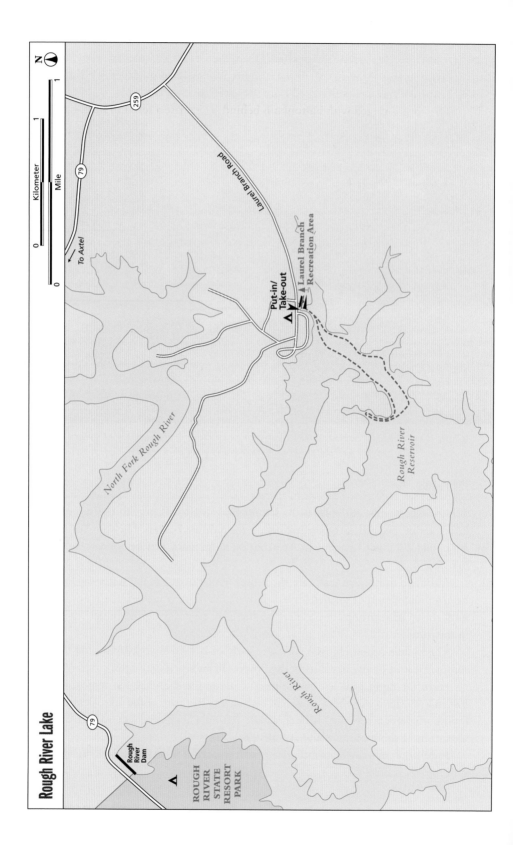

A low, gravel shoreline, often shaded from the heat of the afternoon sun, makes a nice stopping place for a swim in the summer months. The water drops off gradually inside the cove, which is sheltered from the waves of the main lake.

The cove is ringed with buttonbush behind which rise a forest of pine, sycamore, oaks, and other hardwood species. Wildlife is plentiful—even in mid-summer. The lake is home to geese, great blue heron, a variety of ducks, and woodpeckers.

Rough River Lake boasts excellent populations of largemouth and hybrid striped bass, along with bluegill, catfish, crappie, and walleye.

35 Barren River Lake

This loop paddle beginning at the Bailey's Point Campground is in the heart of the lake in a southern bend of the river and takes in the best of what Barren has to offer recreational boaters—fishing, views, wildlife, rock hunting, and swimming. It can easily be extended or shortened.

County: Barren
Start and End: Bailey's Point Campground N 36 52.827', W 86 05.559'
Distance: 3 miles
Float Time: 2.5 hours
Difficulty: Easy to moderate, depending on wind and current near dam
Rapids: None
River Type: Lake
Current: None
River Gradient: None
River Gauge: www.lrl-wc.usace.army.mil/reports/lkreport.html

Lake levels fluctuate. Winter pool is at 528 feet while summer pool is at 552 feet. Flood stage is at 590 feet.
Land Status: Public
Nearest Cities/Towns: Glasgow, Scottsville
Boats Used: Canoe, Kayak, SUP
Season: Any
Fees or Permits: USACE Day-use fee $5, Day-use fee waived if staying at campground. Sites $17–$50.
Maps: USGS Lucas, Austin
Organizations/Contacts: USACE 11088 Finney Road, Glasgow, KY 42141, (270) 646-2055; Daily Lake information line: (270) 646-2122

Getting There

Put-In/Take-Out: From Glasgow, take U.S. 31 E South (Scottsville Road) to Ky. 252 N, follow it for 1.8 miles, then turn right onto Ky. 517, follow it 0.7 mile, and then turn left onto Bailey Point Road. You will reach Bailey's Point Campground in 3 miles. Every loop in the campground has carrydown access. There are a boat ramp and courtesy dock as well, but it is busy with motorized craft.

River Overview

Barren River Lake encompasses more than 10,000 acres and was created in 1964 by the impoundment of the Barren River by the US Army Corps of Engineers as part of the massive Ohio River Basin Flood Control Plan. The Barren River is 135 miles long and the largest tributary to the Green River, which it enters in Warren County.

Native Americans lived, fished, and hunted along the Barren River's floodplain and terraces dating back to as early as 12,000 BC. By AD 900, the Native Americans were farming the fertile valleys, and periodically they burned off parts of the land to provide grasslands for grazing bison. When settlers began arriving in the 1700s, the landscape looked "barren," and the name stuck.

The Paddle

Bailey's Point is located on a peninsula almost directly in the center of the lake directly between the Barren River Lake Dam and the Barren River Lake State Resort Park.

I began from the shoreline below our campsite in the primitive F camping loop. Every loop in the campground offers shore access to campers, and there is a boat ramp located on the western tip of the peninsula, but it is a considerable distance to

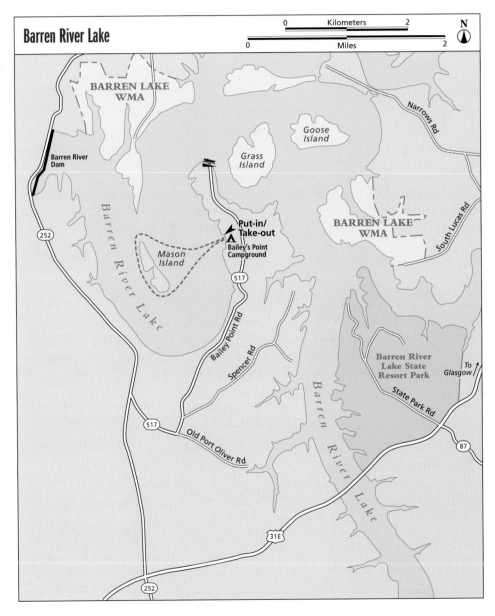

Kayakers on a sunset paddle of Barren River Lake. CARRIE STAMBAUGH

paddle around the tip of the peninsula to where the shoreline access at the campgrounds is located on the eastern facing side.

From the shoreline, we headed directly across the channel of the lake, paddling 0.85 mile to reach the eastern shoreline of Mason Island in the center of this southeasterly bend in the river.

The southern shore, or the "outside" of the bend, is marked by dramatic, steep, rocky cliffs that appear to encircle one. Just beyond the strip of trees that make up the surrounding Barren River Lake Wildlife Management Area are vacation homes and farmland, which one passes on the road to the campground and launch.

Head south toward the southern end of the island, and then turn northward, hugging the island. We stopped on the shore of a cove that almost bisects the island before completing our trip around it. The shoreline is gentle with gravel and rocks, making it a popular swimming spot. (On the day we visited, we shared the cove with two other motorized boats, and upon leaving, we passed a flotilla of kayakers heading into the cove for the same purpose.)

Rounding the northern tip of the island, the shoreline becomes high cliffs of rock. Dozens of birds were roosted in the trees high above the lake, so take caution not to get too close to the shoreline.

A complete circumnavigation of the island is complete at mile 1.9, and crossing back to the campground is an additional 0.8 mile—making the paddle a total distance of 2.7 miles.

Note: Barren River Lakes shores are a rock hounds delight. In addition to a handful of Indian bead fossils, the colloquial name for crinoid fossils, I found a small geode during a quick sweep of the shore on this paddle. (Fossil collecting is not allowed within the boundary of Barren River State Park.)

Fishing is excellent on Barren River Lake. Species include bluegill, catfish, crappie, and six varieties of bass: hybrid, largemouth, smallmouth, spotted, white, and yellow.

Barren River Lake is also a popular destination for birders. Sandhill cranes stop by in January and February during their annual migrations, and the federally endangered whooping crane has also been spotted here, too. Species change throughout the year. Other waterfowl include the aforementioned wood ducks, great blue heron, belted kingfishers, osprey, gulls, terns, egrets, and cormorants. Enthusiasts have tallied sightings of more than 170 species just inside the state park!

36 Gasper River

The Gasper River is a tributary of the Barren River and one of the most scenic waterways in western Kentucky. The river drains the rolling Pennyroyal Hills between Russellville and Bowling Green, flowing over a rock, sand, and clay bottom, around boulders, and through a small gorge with almost vertical-exposed rock walls that in places rise directly from the river's edge. Most of the land surrounding the river is farmland.

County: Warren
Start: Ky. 626 Jackson Bridge
N 37.01305', W 86 36.419'
End: U.S. 231 Bridge
N 37 03.191' W 86 35.792'
Length: 3.5 miles
Float Time: 1 to 2 hours
Difficulty: Moderate, due to rapids and holes
Rapids: I-II
River Type: Rocky, rural waterway
Current: Slow to moderate
River Gradient: 4.8 fpm
River Gauge: There is no gauge on the Gasper. The USGS Gauge at West Fork Drakes Creek can be a good comparison gauge. It should have a minimum reading of 220 cfs.
Land Status: Private
Nearest City/Town: Bowling Green
Boats Used: Canoe, Kayak, SUP
Season: Fall, winter, spring
Fees and Permits: No
Maps: USGS Hadley
Organizations: The Southcentral Kentucky Rivers Blueways Project—Warren County Blueways, www.wku.edu/blueways
  Warren County Parks, www.warrencountyky.gov/parks-and-river-access
Contact/Outfitter: Drakes Creek Canoe LLC, (270) 781-3938, www.drakescreekcanoe.com

Getting There

To Take-out/Shuttle Point: From Bowling Green, take U.S. 231 North for approximately 10 miles to just before the roadway crosses over the Gasper River. The take-out is located on the south of the roadway under the bridge.

To Put-in from Take-out: To reach the put-in, turn around and head south for 0.4 mile on U.S. 231 to the intersection of Ky. 626 on the right. Follow Ky. 626 for 2.1 miles. Park on the north side of KY 626 between a metal fence post and the bridge. There is room for three vehicles. A working farm surrounds this access. Do not park on the south side of Ky. 626 or block farm gates, and do not linger here. The landowner will call authorities.

The Paddle

This is an exciting 3.5-mile float that begins just above the Ky. 626 Bridge and ends at the U.S. 231(Morgantown Road) Bridge near the community of Hadley. If the river is flowing from the buff on the right to the left bank here and you can hear the

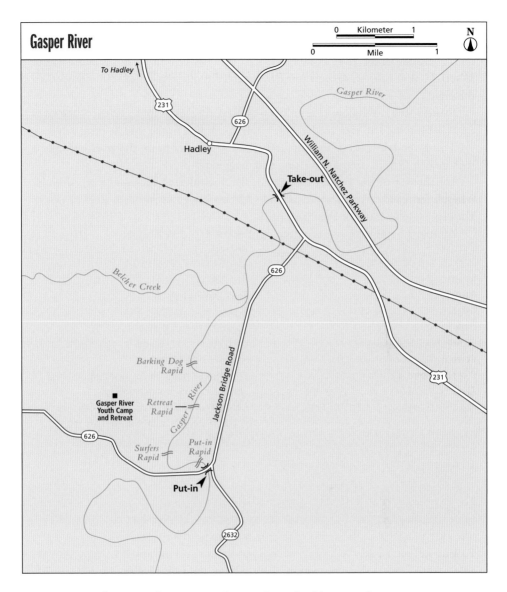

Put-In Rapid roaring downstream, inexperienced whitewater boaters may want to skip this run.

The action begins almost immediately, with the aptly named Put-In Rapid, a Class II rapid of straightforward waves. As the river flows under the Ky. 626 Bridge, at 0.1 mile, it takes a hard left into the rapid. It is followed by what whitewater paddlers call Surfers Rapid, as the Gasper takes a bend to the right at mile marker 0.4.

Another Class II, Surfers Rapid depends on water levels whether there are one or two standing waves that can be "surfed" by eddying out and reentering the wave train.

Following this rapid, at mile 0.6 is the longest and most defined series of standing waves on this paddle. It is known as Retreat Rapid for the Catholic Retreat Center on the left side of the river. For experienced whitewater boaters, this is another spot to surf. Look for the wave/hole just left of center about two-thirds of the way down the rapid.

Retreat Rapid is followed at mile 0.8 by Barking Dog Rapid, created as the river turns hard to the left, and another "play hole" is located in the middle of the river.

This is the last rapid of the trip, and at lower summer flows, the river becomes a rock garden that may require walking and dragging.

For the rest of this paddle, the river is flat, meandering back and forth through tranquil farmland. As you approach mile 3, the river passes beneath a set of power lines, so begin to look for the take-out.

At mile 3.5, the take-out is on the right at the U.S. 231 Bridge.

37 Kentucky Lake

With more than 2,400 miles of shoreline to explore from forty-eight public access areas, there are thousands of paddling options on this lake. This paddle explores a section of the more than 300 miles of undeveloped shoreline along the Land Between the Lakes National Recreation Area near Smith's Bay. It can easily be enlarged, and the put-in and take-out are the same location near a camping area, making this paddle an excellent choice for a camping and canoe trip!

Counties: Trigg, Marshall, Lyon
Start and End: Sugar Bay Ramp
N 36 51.378', W 88 07.635'
Distance: 5.3 miles
Float Time: 3 hours
Rapids: None
River Type: Lake
Current: Slow to moderate in channel
River Gradient: 1 fpm
River Gauge: https://www.tva.gov/Environment/Lake-Levels/Kentucky
Land Status: Public/private
Nearest City/Town: Aurora
Boats Used: Canoe, Kayak, SUP
Season: Any
Fees or Permits: No day use fee. Overnight camping fees are $7 for 3-day permit
Maps: USGS Fairdealing, Fenton
Organizations: Friends of Land Between the Lakes, 345 Maintenance Drive, Golden Pond, KY 42211, (800) 455-5897, www.friendsoflbl.org

Contacts: US Forest Service Land Between The Lakes National Recreation Area, 100 Van Morgan Drive, Golden Pond, KY 42211; (800) 525-7077, Lblinfo@Fs.Fed.Us or www.landbetweenthelakes.us/visit/contact
Tennessee Valley Authority, www.tva.gov
Outfitters: Canoe and Kayak Rentals are seasonal.
Green Turtle Bay Boat Rentals, 263 Turtle Bay Drive, Grand Rivers, KY 42045, (800) 498-0428
Lynnhurst Family Resort, 270 Lynnhurst Drive, Murray, KY 42071, (270) 436-2345
LBL Kayak and Canoe Rental, 1506 Donelson Parkway, Dover, TN 37058, (931) 627-4319
Lake Barkley Marina, 4200 State Park Road, Cadiz, KY 42211, (270) 924-6081
Cedar Knob Resort, 1434 Cedar Knob Road, Benton, KY 42025, (270) 354-8475

Getting There

To Put-in/Take-out: Sugar Bay Campground Boat Ramp. From Aurora, take U.S. 68 East. Turn left at its intersection with Ky. 80. Travel 3.9 miles, crossing the Eggner's Ferry Bridge, then take the exit on the right to Woodlands Trace/Ky. 453 (Grand Rivers, KY / Dover, TN). Turn left at the bottom of the ramp. Follow Ky. 453 North for 5 miles, and then turn left onto Forest Service Road 140. Follow it 2.2 miles to the campground and boat ramp.

Kentucky Lake is a massive body of water that stretches 184 miles through Kentucky and Tennessee. At 160,309 acres it has 2,064 miles of shoreline, has a flood storage capacity of more than 4 million acre-feet, and is the largest man-made lake east of the Mississippi River.

The lake was created by the impoundment of the Tennessee River by the Tennessee Valley Authority. It was initiated as part of President Franklin D. Roosevelt's New Deal following devastating flooding in 1937. Construction on the Kentucky Dam, located 22 miles south of the mouth of the Tennessee River at Paducah, began in 1938 and concluded in 1944.

LAND BETWEEN THE LAKES NATIONAL RECREATION AREA

The Land Between the Lakes (LBL) National Recreation Area was established in 1963, setting aside more than 170,000 acres between Lake Barkley and Kentucky Lake for outdoor recreation. It is the nation's largest inland peninsula. The LBL varies from 1 to 9 miles wide and is 40 miles long from its southern region in Tennessee to its northern edge in Kentucky, just below the canal connecting the lakes.

It includes more than 300 miles of natural shoreline, in addition to more than 500 miles of hiking, biking, horseback, and off-road trails. LBL also offers geocaching with five heritage geocache sites within the boundaries of the recreation area.

The 200 miles of paved roads offer easy scenic driving, but there are 200 more miles of unpaved forest service roads to explore too. Woodlands Trace National Scenic Byway traverses the LBL from north to south between U.S. 62 and U.S. 68, respectively.

There is an abundance of public recreation facilities, including more than 1,400 campsites in twenty-one different campgrounds ranging from developed to primitive. There are twenty-six boat ramps and five environmental education facilities, a planetarium and observatory, and The Homeplace, which is a circa 1850s living museum and working farm. There are also the remains of two iron-stack furnaces within the park, including the 35-foot-high Center Furnace near the Woodlands Nature Station.

A 700-acre fenced bison and elk habitat is accessible to closed vehicles and features a 3.5-mile paved loop road. More than 240 species of birds have been seen and recorded within the recreation area, making it a destination for birders. LBL is also popular with hunters for deer, turkey, waterfowl, and other small game.

The area draws an estimated 1.5 million visitors annually.

A view south down Kentucky Lake to the distant Eggner's Ferry Bridge. CARRIE STAMBAUGH

The project inundated the towns of Birmingham, Kentucky, and Johnsonville and Springfield, Tennessee. In all, more than 2,600 families and 3,300 graves had to be relocated for the project along with 365 miles of roads and a railroad.

According to the Tennessee Valley Authority, Kentucky Dam provides flood protection for 6 million acres of land in the Ohio and Mississippi River Basins. The five turbines in the hydroelectric plant at Kentucky Dam Powerhouse generate more than 1.3 billion kilowatt-hours of electricity annually.

The waterway is also a major navigational channel. Part of the 21-state inland waterway system, it is also connected to nearby Lake Barkley (Cumberland River) by a mile-long canal. An estimated 31 million tons of freight are moved through the waterway annually, with more than 2,000 barges passing through the lock at the eastern end of the Kentucky Dam monthly.

Kentucky Lake parallels Lake Barkley for more than 50 miles, and in between the two bodies of water lies the Land Between the Lakes National Recreation Area.

The Paddle

The paddle starts at the Sugar Bay Ramp, which is tucked in a quiet bay away from the main body of the lake. From the ramp, head to the right toward the main lake. In

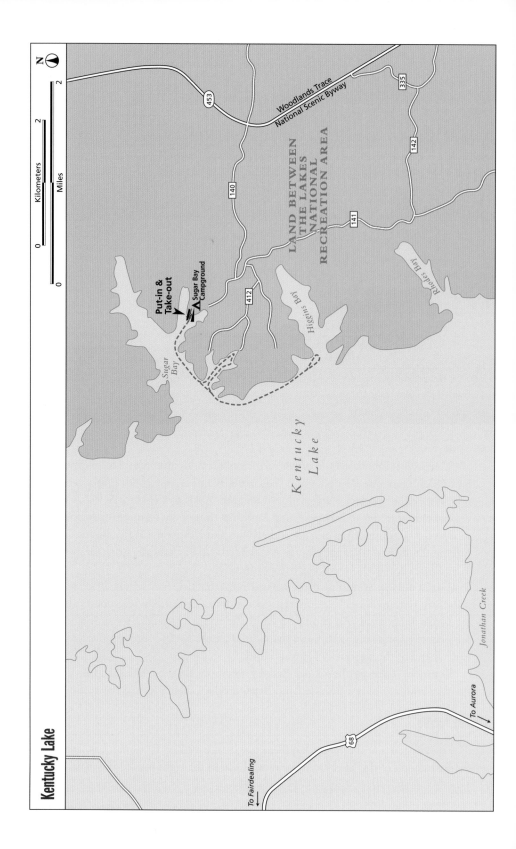

Kentucky Lake

Put-in & Take-out

Sugar Bay Campground

Sugar Bay

Higgins Bay

Rhodes Bay

Kentucky Lake

Woodlands Trace National Scenic Byway

LAND BETWEEN THE LAKES NATIONAL RECREATION AREA

Jonathan Creek

To Aurora

To Fairdealing

453

335

142

140

141

412

68

N

Kilometers

Miles

0   2

0   2

0.1 mile, follow the shoreline as it curves to the left, and in 0.4 mile, the main lake comes into view.

Reaching the main lake at mile 1.4, continue to hug the left bank as you head south down the main lake. The distant Eggner's Ferry Bridge, carrying traffic on U.S. 68 comes into view in the distance. The shoreline varies from sand and gravel banks to rocky ledges and boulder-strewn. The shoreline to the east is heavily wooded.

Stay to the left bank, where the current is less strong and you are well out of the way of the large commercial vessels—tows often consisting of more than a dozen barges. There are often lots of pleasure boats on the water as well, so be sure to watch for them and angle your craft into the waves to avoid flipping from their wakes.

At mile 1.8, you reach the mouth of North Higgins Bay. The bay is shallow with large boulders marking the entrance. Continue to hug the left—now north shore—as you enter the bay. At mile 2, there is a nice gravel beach to land and take an afternoon swim in the clear waters.

After continuing into the bay, we decided to turn around and head back toward Sugar Bay at mile 2.8. Retracing our paddle, continuing to hug the shoreline now on our right, we entered Sugar Bay. On the return trip, we spotted several double-crested cormorants perched on a driftwood tree in their signature spread-wing posture.

At mile 3.5, we made a right turn, to the south, to explore a small side bay off the main one, reaching the back of it at mile 4. The water was only several inches deep and the lakebed muddy.

This is a good area to watch out for bald eagles; often they can be seen eating along the shoreline, sitting in treetops, or soaring overhead. There are also other birds along the shoreline as well. On this trip, we spotted a pair of bald eagles eating dead fish along the shore. A large swath of open, grassy bank in the cove would make an excellent camping spot. There were large cypress trees along the shoreline here as well.

Leaving, we headed back to the main branch of Sugar Bay, making a right when we reached it at mile 4.5 and paddled back to the boat ramp, the second bay we reached on the right. We arrived at the ramp at mile 5.3.

38 Lake Barkley

This paddle explores the Honker Bay Recreation Area of Lake Barkley, which is surrounded by the protected Land Between the Lakes Area. It is a popular nature area where dozens of species of birds can often be seen. On this paddle, we travel north, reaching a point on the main lake before turning around and returning. Again, this paddle can easily be extended and would make an excellent canoe camping trip.

County: Lyon
Start and End: Honker Bay Ramp
N 36 54.656', W 88 01.391'
Distance: 4 miles
Float Time: 3 hours
Difficulty: Moderate, due to distance on unprotected water
Rapids: None
River Type: Lake
Current: Moderate
River Gradient: 1 fpm
River Gauge: https://www.tva.gov/Environment/Lake-Levels/Barkley
Land Status: Public/private
Nearest City/Town: Aurora
Boats Used: Canoe, Kayak, SUP
Season: Spring, summer, fall. The area is closed from November 1 to March 15.
Fees or Permits: No day use fee. Overnight camping permit is $7 for a 3-day pass.
Maps: USGS Mont, www.landbetweenthelakes.us/visit/maps

Organizations: Friends of Land Between the Lakes, 345 Maintenance Drive, Golden Pond, KY 42211, (800) 455-5897, www.friendsoflbl.org
Contacts: US Forest Service Land Between the Lakes National Recreation Area, 100 Van Morgan Drive, Golden Pond, KY 42211, (800) 525-7077, Lblinfo@Fs.Fed.Us or www.landbetweenthelakes.us/visit/contact
Outfitters: Canoe and Kayak Rentals are seasonal.

Green Turtle Bay Boat Rentals, 263 Turtle Bay Drive, Grand Rivers, KY 42045, (800) 498-0428

Lynnhurst Family Resort, 270 Lynnhurst Drive, Murray, KY 42071, (270) 436-2345

LBL Kayak and Canoe Rental, 1506 Donelson Parkway, Dover Tennessee

Lake Barkley Marina, 4200 State Park Road, Cadiz, KY 42211, (270) 924-6081

Cedar Knob Resort, 1434 Cedar Knob Road, Benton, KY 42025, (270) 354-8475

Getting There

To Put-in/Take-out: To the Honker Bay Day Use Area Boat Ramp from Hopkinsville, take U.S. 68 West (Cadiz Road) for 30 miles, crossing Lake Barkley/Cumberland River on the Lawrence Memorial Bridge. At the foot of the bridge, make a right onto Forest Service Road 134. In 8.3 miles, turn right onto Forest Service Road 135. After 2.1 miles, turn left onto Forest Service Road 138, and in 0.5 mile, make another left just before a gate across the road. The ramp will be on the lake (left) side at the very end of the road. Parking for up to ten vehicles is available.

River Overview

Lake Barkley is 57,900 acres at summer pool and boasts just over a thousand miles of shoreline in Kentucky and Tennessee. The lake is the last in a series of impoundments along the Cumberland River and its tributaries. It is named in honor of a Paducah native, the late Alben W. Barkley, who served as the 35th US vice president and as a US senator.

The lake was created when the Barkley Dam was constructed between 1957 and 1966. It impounds 118 miles of the Cumberland River from mile 30.6 above the confluence of the river and the Ohio River to Cheatham Dam at mile 148.7. It is the westernmost impoundment along the 688-mile river that flows west from its headwaters in southeast Kentucky through Kentucky and then into northern Tennessee before turning and flowing north back into Kentucky and, eventually, emptying into the Ohio River upstream of the Tennessee River.

Lake Barkley parallels Kentucky Lake for more than 50 miles; in between the two bodies of water lies the Land Between the Lakes National Recreation Area. The two are connected by a mile-long canal located south of the respective Kentucky and Barkley Dams.

The Paddle

Honker Bay Recreation Area is located within the Land Between the Lakes National Recreation Area and is part of a designated forest service wildlife refuge for migrating bird species, making it an excellent destination for paddling and bird watching. Be on the lookout for eagles, ospreys, Canada geese, great and snowy egrets, and wood ducks on the open water and scan the shoreline for glimpses of green herons, eastern kingbirds, warblers, and more.

The ramp is located just beyond the dam for Honker Lake on a narrow peninsula separating the bay from the main lake. Leaving the ramp, head north, hugging the eastern bank of the peninsula.

At mile 0.75, you will reach the northern tip of the peninsula; angle left to continue paddling northwest across the open mouth of the bay toward its northern shore. You are paralleling the main channel of Lake Barkley. On our visit a flock of white birds was floating at the mouth, although we never got close enough to see exactly what they were, I suspect they were egrets. This stretch of water can get wind-whipped and choppy, be sure to pay attention to the direction of the waves and make adjustments to your heading.

At mile 1.6, pass by a small island. We noticed a large osprey nest at the top of a tall dead standing tree here, and we did catch a glimpse of one of the birds returning to it with a fish, although we didn't see its hatchlings!

At mile 1.7 reach the northern tip of the bay and continue north along the shoreline for a tenth of a mile to reach a gravel shoreline. This is a great spot to take a break, stretch your legs, and explore the coast. There were lots of freshwater mussel

Paddlers head across Honker Bay, a designated U.S. Forest Service Wildlife Refuge. Bev Braun

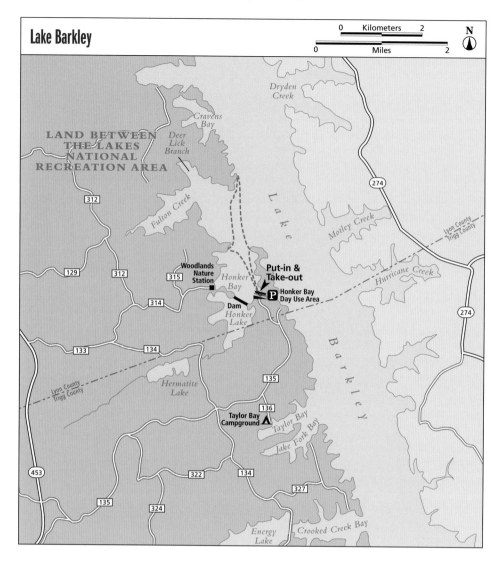

and clam shells along the shore, in addition to large rocks with a variety of fossils. On the day we visited, the sun was shining, and the breeze off the main lake was cooling.

Back in the boat, head back toward the ramp. This time, however, hug the shore to your right as you round the tip, heading southeast around the tip of the shoreline, and enter the bay. Pass behind the small island this time. Note that there are a number of standing tree stumps beneath the water here, so be aware. There is also a crosscurrent here, which can create waves that push your boat out toward the main lake. Be sure to head far enough into the bay to get out of the current.

Head toward a point of land sticking out on the western shore, passing by the wide mouth of a bay marking where two creeks enter the lake on your right (western side). The first bay that heads north is Deer Lick Branch, the second is Fulton Creek, which flows west to east. These bays, along with Honker Bay, are part of a series of US Forest Service Wildlife Refuges in LBL and closed to the public between November 1 and March 15 to provide habitat to migrating bird species. A portion of the main channel of Lake Barkley in this area is a US Fish and Wildlife Refuge and is also closed at that same time. (The navigational channel next to the eastern shore remains open.) If you want to extend your paddle from the one described here, this is the spot to do it. Turn right to explore these bays.

To remain in Honker Bay, paddle across the open stretch of water here toward the dam in the distance. Reach the aforementioned point of the land, a small peninsula, at mile 2.5. Adjust your heading to aim for the boat ramp to the east side of the dam, and again paddle across the open bay, reaching the ramp at mile 3.5. An easy way to extend this paddle would be to hug the western shoreline for a further distance before crossing to the boat ramp.

39 Little River

This is a loop paddle on the Little River through the heart of Lake Barkley State Resort Park, where the river flows into Lake Barkley. Much of the surrounding shoreline is public property—except for a stretch of the northern shoreline. The park is a great "home base" for a camping and canoe trip.

County: Trigg
Start and End: Lake Barkley State Park Boat Ramp/Marina
N 36 51.205', W 87 56.578'
Distance: 5.4 miles
Float Time: 4 hours
Difficulty: Moderate, due to motorized boat traffic
Rapids: None
River Type: Flood control lake
Current: Slow
River Gradient: 1 foot per mile
River Gauge: https://www.tva.gov/Environment/Lake-Levels/Barkley

Land Status: Public/private
Nearest City/Town: Cadiz
Boats Used: Canoe, Kayak, SUP
Season: Spring, summer, fall
Fees or Permits: No day use fees
Maps: USGS Canton, Lake Barkley State Resort Park Facilities Map
Organizations/Contacts: Lake Barkley State Resort Park, 3500 State Park Road, Cadiz, KY 42211, (270) 924-1131, www.parks.ky.gov/resortparks/lake-barkely
Outfitters: Lake Barkley Marina, 4200 State Park Road, Cadiz, KY 42211, (270) 924-6081. Kayak and Canoe Rentals are seasonal.

Getting There

To Put-in/Take-out: From Hopkinsville, take U.S. 68 West for 22 miles. Turn right onto Ky. 1489, follow it 3.4 miles, and then turn right onto State Park Road. Follow for 0.7 mile, then turn left, following signs to boat ramp/marina.

River Overview

The Little River meets Lake Barkley west of Cadiz. The upper Little River is noted for its winding course and virgin, timber-lined banks. The river starts in southern Christian County and flows north through Trigg County and the town of Cadiz before entering Lake Barkley—a dammed pool of the Cumberland River. Much of the southern bank of the river here, along with a large island in the channel of the river is part of Lake Barkley State Resort Park.

The Paddle

The river is wide for much of this stretch, narrowing as it circles a small island, which is the destination of this paddle.

Beginning at the Lake Barkley boat ramp and marina, first head straight out into the lake to get "behind" the first of three small islands before turning right to head

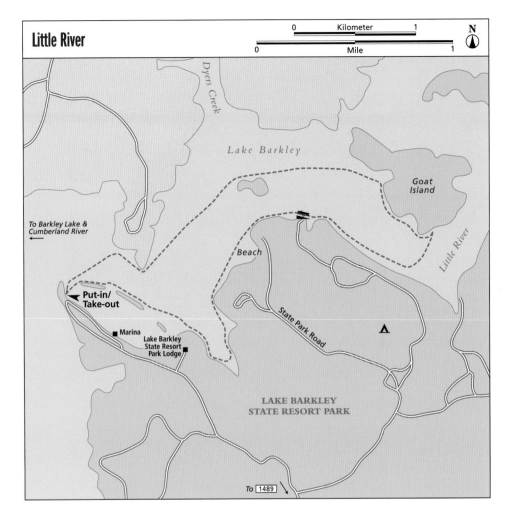

0   Kilometer   1

0   Mile   1

N

Dyers Creek

Lake Barkley

Goat Island

Little River

To Barkley Lake & Cumberland River

Beach

Put-in/ Take-out

Marina

State Park Road

Lake Barkley State Resort Park Lodge

LAKE BARKLEY STATE RESORT PARK

To 1489

southeast or "upriver." Be sure to watch for motorized traffic in the area, don't always count on these crafts to give you the deserved right-of-way. There is little current here due to the slack waters of Lake Barkley, but the wind can whip up swells.

Reach the far tip of the last island at mile 0.6; Lake Barkley Lodge is straight ahead on the southern shore. The structure made of glass, stone, and beams of Douglas fir and western cedar is striking. Continue toward the lodge, passing the shore directly beneath it at mile 0.7. Continue straight to explore a quiet bay within the park property, passing its walkways and a small playground. This is an idle zone, so there are no fast, motorized crafts to contend with. The cove is full of wildlife. I've often spotted deer along the shore and many species of birds, including great blue and green herons, snowy egrets, many ducks, and common loons.

The Little River offers quiet paddling upriver of Lake Barkley. BEV BRAUN

Reach the back of the cove at mile 1, continuing to hug the shore on the right-hand side. Continue around the bay back toward the main channel of the Little River. At the end of the cove, at mile 1.4, turn right to head further upriver.

As you round the point here, you will see the swimming beach ahead of you on the southern shore of the river. This is a popular spot for sunbathers during the summer. Pass by it at mile 1.8. The river enters a right turn here. Notice a small boat ramp on the southern shore at mile 2.1.

As the river reaches the apex of its turn at mile 2.7, cross to the island, being on the lookout for motorized craft as you turn northward. You should reach the island at mile 2.9. The gently sloping gravel shoreline here is an excellent place to land for lunch and to explore the small island.

Head back toward the boat ramp, hugging the island to head north around its western side. Reach a small cove along the island's shore at mile 3.4. This is a favorite place for birds, and we saw several great blue heron fishing alongside egrets.

Leaving the island, head west or downstream back toward the harbor. At mile 4, pass to the north of a small island, being sure to watch for stumps sticking up just below the water's surface. After passing the island, begin to angle slightly southward. At mile 4.9, round a point directly across from the islands in front of the marina.

Again, watching for motorized craft, paddle south across the channel and aim for the westernmost edge of the last island. Reach the boat ramp at mile 5.4.

40 Clarks River

This paddle is an out-and-back loop exploring the heart of the Clarks River National Wildlife Refuge on the East Fork of the Clarks River. The paddle explores an area that includes Coon Pond just upriver from the Burkholder Deadening, which can be accessed from the same put-in as this paddle. It is best paddled in the cool seasons, particularly after the first frost in fall because it can grow quite buggy during warm, humid weather. In the fall the foliage is particularly striking.

Fishing in the Clarks River is excellent. The habitat is perfect for large spotted and largemouth bass along with bluegill and crappie.

County: Marshall

Start and End: Milliken Bridge Ramp, off Milliken Mill Road
N 36 54.390', W 88 24.641'

Distance: 3 miles

Float Time: 2 to 3 hours

Rapids: None

River Type: Windy river with abundant oxbows and swamp areas

Current: Slow

River Gradient: 2 feet per mile

River Gauge: USGS Gauge is Clarks River at Almo. The minimum reading should be 165 cfs. Stay off the river if gauges show it is rising.

Land Status: Public

Nearest City/Town: Benton

Boats Used: Canoe, Kayak (SUP not recommended due to presence of poisonous snakes)

Season: Fall, winter, spring, early summer

Fees or Permits: No

Maps: USGS Elva; Clarks River National Wildlife Refuge map

Organizations:

Contacts/Outfitters: Clarks River National Wildlife Refuge, 91 US Highway 641 North, PO Box 89, Benton, KY 42025, (270) 527-5770, fw4rwclarksriver@fws.gov, US Fish & Wildlife Service, (800) 344-WILD

Getting There

To Put-in/Take-out: From Benton, take U.S. 641/North Main Street to Ky. 795 North for approximately 2 miles. Turn left, following Ky. 795 for 4.5 miles. Turn left onto Milliken Mill Lane. In 1.3 miles, the road crosses over the Clarks River; the access road to the boat ramp is on the left immediately after the bridge.

River Overview

The Clark River is 66.7 miles long and located in the Jackson Purchase Area of western Kentucky. It is named for William Clark, of the Lewis and Clark Expedition. The river drains portions of Marshall, Graves, and McCracken County southeast of Paducah, emptying into the Tennessee River east of the city. There are two main forks of the river, the East and West Fork, which join together at Oaks Station in McCracken County. It is one of the very few rivers in the region that has not been

Clarks River offers paddling in a unique ecosystem of slow moving water, called sloughs, that are surrounded by bald cypress trees. CARRIE STAMBAUGH

dammed or channelized and is prone to seasonal flooding, creating additional swamp and wetlands.

The Clarks River National Wildlife Refuge was established in 1997 under the Emergency Wetland Resources Act, with the first tract of land acquired in 1998, to preserve one of the last remaining bottomland hardwood forests in the region. It is the only National Wildlife Refuge fully within Kentucky and encompasses more than 8,500 acres along 40 miles of the East Fork. Land is still being acquired for the refuge, which has a proposed acquisition boundary of 18,000 acres.

The river flows between steep, muddy banks forested by cypress, Tupelo gum, sycamore, overcup oaks, willows, maples, ash, sweet gum, and elm, along with other varieties of oaks. The soil here is enriched by seasonal flooding, resulting in a diverse ecosystem.

Wildlife is abundant here and includes more than 200 species of migrating songbirds and waterfowl, along with fish, amphibians, mussels, and clams. A variety of mammals live along the river, and it isn't uncommon to spot river otter swimming in pairs or small groups. The river is also home to the cottonmouth or water moccasin, one of three poisonous snakes found in Kentucky.

The Paddle

This loop paddle is located in the heart of the Clarks River National Wildlife Refuge where there is the easiest access to the river. The paddle can easily be extended, in either direction, either up or down river. Be aware, however, that the river is prone to flooding, and frequent logjams may block access. Portaging can be tricky because of the swampy nature of the forest and often because banks are steep and muddy.

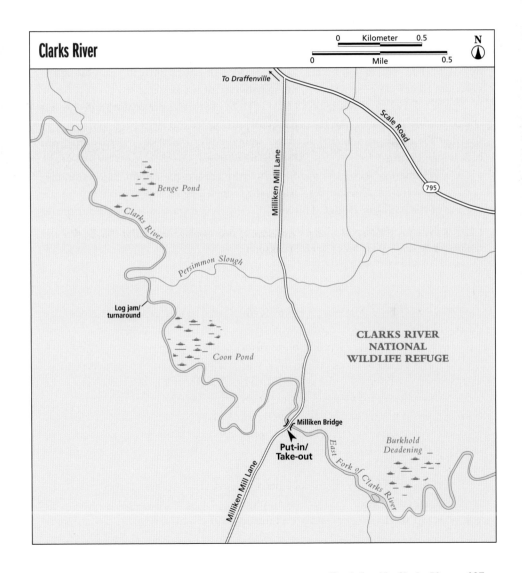

To begin, from the boat ramp, head down river or left, immediately crossing under the bridge. The river immediately begins a turn to the right, paralleling the road for the first 0.2 mile as it heads north. The river then turns away from the road as it heads south. At mile 0.5, it enters the first of two curves to the right. The first is gentle, and the second at mile 0.6 is sharp as it heads northeast again.

At mile 0.7, it takes a left turn to again head west for a tenth of a mile before turning to the left again and heading south before turning northward again. At mile 0.9, enter Coon Pond. This area of swampy wetlands is a good representation of the region. During high water, boaters can float through stands of cypress and other hardwoods; during low water, stick to the main channel of the pond. It is roughly two-tenths of a mile directly across the pond, but a more circuitous path is recommended, bearing to the left. The exit to the pond is on the northwest side, almost exactly across from the entrance.

Reach it at mile 1.3. The river continues its overall northwesterly path, curving first right then left. At mile 1.5, Persimmon Slough enters from the east. Slough—pronounced like slew—is a slow-moving tributary of water.

Past the slough, the river makes a hard left. On my paddle, the river at mile 1.6 was chocked with logs, forcing us to turn around and retrace our steps back to the put-in. (Beyond the curve, at mile 1.8, the river straightens out a bit as it heads northwest into Benge Pond.)

It is possible to extend the paddle further by passing the put-in and continuing upstream toward the Burkholder Deadening, which begins approximately 0.6 mile upriver of the Milliken Bridge. This area of roughly a thousand acres of bottomland wetland forest. Seasonal flooding keeps the forest floor relatively clean and open, providing an accurate representation of what the pioneers first journeying to the Jackson Purchase would have encountered.

Resources and References

American Canoe Association: www.americancanoe.org
Founded in 1880, the American Canoe Association (ACA) is a national nonprofit serving the broader paddling public by providing education related to all aspects of paddling. It also provides stewardship support and sanctions programs and events to promote competition as well as exploration and recreation.

American Whitewater: www.americanwhitewater.org
Founded in 1954, American Whitewater is a national nonprofit whose mission is "to conserve and restore America's whitewater resources and to enhance opportunities to enjoy them." A member organization, it includes one hundred affiliate paddling clubs across the nation.

Bluegrass Wildwater Association: www.bluegrasswildwater.org
Founded in 1976, the 200-plus member club is based in Lexington, Kentucky. The organization operates Spring Beginners Clinic in mid-May on the Russell Fork of the Big Sandy. In addition, its website is a great place for information. Its winter pool roll sessions are popular with both seasoned veterans and new beginners.

Clark, Thomas D. *The Kentucky* (1942), J. J. Little and Ives Company: New York.

Dick, David and Lalie Dick, *Rivers of Kentucky* (2001), Plum Lick Publishing, Inc: North Middleton, KY.

Kentucky Department of Fish and Wildlife Resources, "Blue Water Trail Series," Frankfort, KY.

Kleber, John E., *The Kentucky Encyclopedia* (1992, third printing), University of Kentucky Press: Lexington, KY.

National Geographic Maps, *National Geographic Road Atlas Adventure Edition, United States, Mexico, Canada* (2012), National Geographic Maps, Globe Turner LLC. and Mapping Specialties, Ltd.: Washington, DC.

Sehlinger, Bob and Johnny Molloy, *Canoeing and Kayaking Kentucky* (2017, sixth edition), Menasha Ridge Press: Birmingham, AL.

Rennick, Robert M., *Kentucky Place Names* (1984), University of Kentucky Press: Lexington, KY.

US Bureau of Transportation Statistics: www.bts.gov.

Paddle Index

About the Author

Carrie "Mudfoot" Stambaugh is an award-winning multimedia journalist and adventurer based in eastern Kentucky. In addition to *Paddling Kentucky*, she is also the author of *Hiking Kentucky: A Guide to 80 of Kentucky's Greatest Hiking Adventures*. She is the cohost of the Kentucky travel adventure show *Downstream*.

Her love of the outdoors began as a small child, maybe even as an infant when her parents put her in a backpack and took her to the top of the Great Smoky Mountains. A six-week adventure trip in the Northwest at age 16 with Wilderness Ventures nurtured her passion to hike, camp, climb, paddle, and explore the natural world.

She earned her trail-name Mudfoot during a thru-hike attempt of the Appalachian Trail, which she and her husband Carl "The Fireman" Stambaugh undertook in 2010. The couple live off-grid in a remote cabin in the hills of Elliott County, Kentucky.

Carrie writes for a variety of publications, including newspapers, magazines, and websites. To read more of her travel writing and watch episodes of *Downstream*, visit www.CarrieStambaugh.com.